RIVER ROADS TO FREEDOM

FUGITIVE SLAVE NOTICES
AND
SHERIFF NOTICES
FOUND IN ILLINOIS SOURCES

Compiled by

Helen Cox Tregillis

HERITAGE BOOKS
2012

HERITAGE BOOKS

AN IMPRINT OF HERITAGE BOOKS, INC.

Books, CDs, and more—Worldwide

For our listing of thousands of titles see our website
at
www.HeritageBooks.com

Published 2012 by
HERITAGE BOOKS, INC.
Publishing Division
100 Railroad Ave. #104
Westminster, Maryland 21157

Other Heritage Books by the author:

*Ancestors: A Teaching Story Using the Families of Cox, Hayes,
Hulse, Range, Worley and Others with Suggested Lessons*

Central Illinois Chronicles, Volumes 1-3

Illinois, the 14th Colony: French Period

Indians of Illinois

People and Rural Schools of Shelby County, Illinois

*River Roads to Freedom: Fugitive Slave Notices and
Sheriff Notices Found in Illinois Sources*

The Native Tribes of Ohio

International Standard Book Numbers
Paperbound: 978-1-55613-120-2
Clothbound: 978-0-7884-9164-1

TABLE OF CONTENTS

Prologue

Index

PROLOGUE

In the beginning, I did not realize that the State of Illinois, indeed, had a definite "Black Code" before the Civil War. Illinois had been admitted as a free state to the Union that prohibited slavery, but that did not deter her from having limitations within her own borders.

The fugitive, sheriff notices were obtained from newspaper microfilm available from the Illinois State Historical Library, Springfield, Illinois. The preserved issues are not complete in years by any means, especially many of the early years and Civil War years.

Those newspapers checked were the cities located on Illinois boundaries. For example, Alton, IL had very incomplete files; two years--1836-1837-- resulted with no notices, even though the town was an entering point for the "underground railroad." Beardstown, IL only had 1848-1849 as the earliest available year, and again the files for the 1850's were very incomplete. Belleville, IL over a span of four years provided few notices. Cairo, IL, likewise, had very, very incomplete files. Chester, IL, another gateway city for the "underground railroad," had no early complete year. Edwardsville, IL, again, had very little complete in the 1850's or 1860's. Kaskaskia, IL provided notices for the years 1816 - 1820. Kaskaskia, of course, did not have a newspaper much longer after that. Quincy, IL, another gateway city for the "underground", did not have complete files. Shawneetown, IL provided notices for years 1819 to 1850; 1850's and 1860's were very incomplete. Springfield, IL for a span of three years--1831-1834--gave few notices.

Since the Illinois fugitive notices included physical descriptions, there can be no doubt in many cases of the treatment of many of the slaves. Many of them did have whip marks on their backs which were affirmed by the sheriffs or authorities who took them into custody.

Many of the fugitives were also mulatto; that by this time after the turn of the 19th century, they were third or fourth generation mulatto. Amazingly, the adjective "bright" was only used to describe the mulatto, not the black. And, "boy" was used even beyond the age of 35.

Also, in examining these notices, it is apparent that a system must have existed before 1830 for the movement of fugitives from the south to the north, as one authority discovered written directions from Florence, Alabama to Detroit, Michigan among the possessions of a fugitive.

Two rivers, the Tennessee and the Cumberland, played a significant role in the fugitive movement from the south to the north.

ILLINOIS AND THE BLACK LAWS
CHAPTER ONE

Illinois entered the union as a free state in 1818, but -- it was not free for any black or person of color.

The Ordinance passed by the Continental Congress on 13 July 1787 "enacted that slavery and involuntary servitude, except as punishment for crimes, should be prohibited forever in the Northwest Territory."(Mather 113-114)

In 1793 Congress accepted federal responsibility for the capture of fugitives by passing a Fugitive Slave Act.(Hart 156) That law or provision allowed a slave owner to reclaim a runaway negro in any state in the union by a mere decision of a local judge, without jury trial.(Muzzey 250)

The Fugitive Slave Act of that date, 1793, essentially had four parts:

"(a) When any white person claimed a runaway slave as his, or her slave, Federal commissioners were promptly to capture the runaway and hand him (or her) over to the one making such claim.

(b) The Commissioners were given authority to call on all citizens to help them make such captures.

(c) Anyone refusing to help or who in any other way assisted the negro to escape, was to be severely punished by fine and imprisonment.

(d) The negro's own testimony as to whether or not he was the claimnant's slave was to be of no value whatever."(Thwaites 312)

By September 1807 when Illinois was part of the Indiana Territory, the general assembly at Vincennes passed "an act concerning the introduction of negroes and mulattoes into this territory." The act essentially read:

"Sec. 1: It shall and may be lawful for any person, being the owner of any negroes or mulattoes of and above the age of 15 years, and owing service and labor as slaves in any of the States and territories of the United States, or for any citizen of the United States or territories purchasing the same, to bring the said negroes or mulattoes into this territory."(Davidson 314)

"The other sections of the act were all in harmony with the purpose to introduce, maintain and protect slavery in Illinois by defiance of the ordinance of 1787. Slavery was thus not only introduced, but made hereditary, by imposing upon the children born under it the obligation to serve the owners of their parents until 28 and 30 years....

After the organization of the Illinois territory in 1809, the governor and judges adopted the same act as the law of Illinois, and upon the assembling of the first legislature at Kaskaskia, it was, Dec. 13, 1812, readopted-...."(Davidson 315)

Thus, after the question of the state's creation, it entered the union as a free state. However, many residents, including the legislators, were southern in origin and took measures to protect themselves from contact from negroes or runaways into their newly created state.

At the second session of the first general assembly of Illinois from January to March 1819, with Lt. Gov. Pierre Menard presiding over the senate and John Messinger presiding over the house, they adopted a code of laws copied chiefly from the Virginia and Kentucky statutes, including the law concerning negroes and mulattoes.(Bateman)

Such senators as Thomas Cox, pioneer from Union County, were zealous advocates for slavery in Illinois. There were 14 senators and 28 representatives, a majority of which adopted and approved the "black laws."(Clayton 190)

Those laws adopted the 30 March 1819 at that second session by the first general assembly of Illinois were:

"AN ACT respecting free Negroes, Mulattoes, Servants and Slaves

Sec. 1. Be it enacted by the people of the state of Illinois represented in the general assembly, That from and after the passage of this act, no black or mulatto person shall be permitted to settle or reside in this state, unless he or she shall first produce a certificate, signed by some judge or clerk of some

2

court in the United States, of his or her actual freedom; which certificate shall have the seal of such court affixed to it; on producing the same to the clerk of the circuit court of the county in which he shall intend to settle, it shall be the duty of such clerk to make an entry thereof, and endorse a certificate on the original certificate, stating the time the same was entered in his office, and the name and description of the person producing the same; after which it shall be lawful for such free negro or mulatto to reside in this state.

[For an example of a certificate of freedom, in the Shelby County, Ill. Deed Record Book 10, page 297: "Know all men by these presents that whereas I George N. Hanson did in the year, 1829 in the county of Russell and state of Virginia, purchase at the sale of the slaves and property belonging to the estate of David Hanson, Sen., Decd., a certain Negro man named Jack and by virtue of said purchase the said Negro man became my lawful property, and whereas I brought said Negro Jack or John (who now calls himself John Hanson) to the state of Illinois in the year 1829 and he has ever since been living in this State, and by virtue of the laws of this State is now entitled to all the privileges of a free man of color. I do hereby relinquish all my right title and claim to him as a slave and do hereby certify he is by virtue of these presents forever free from the claims of myself, my heirs or assigns and entitled to all the rights and privileges of a free man of color. In testimony whereof I have hereunto set my hand and affixed my seal, this 13th day of October, 1846. G.M. Hanson (seal). State of Illinois Coles County, S.S. I, Nathan Ellington, Clerk of the Circuit Court within and for said County do certify that this day George M. Hanson whose signature appears to the within instrument and acknowledged it to be his act and deed for the use and purposes therein contained in testimony, whereof I have hereunto set my hand and affixed the seal of said Court at Charleston, this 15th day of October, 1846. Nathan Ellington, Clerk." The John Hanson family were in Shelby Co., IL 1850.]

3

Sec. 2. And be it further enacted, That it shall be the duty of all free negroes and mulattoes, who shall come to reside in this state after the first day of June next, and having a family of his or her own, and having a certificate as mentioned in the first section of this act, to give to the clerk of the circuit court at the time of making an entry of his certificate, a description, with the name and ages of his, her or their family, which shall be stated by the clerk in the entry made by him of such certificate; and the clerk shall also state the same on the original certificate: Provided however, That nothing contained in this or the preceding section of this act, shall be construed to prevent the overseers of the poor in any township, from causing any such free negro or mulatto to be removed who shall come into this state contrary to the provisions of the act concerning the poor.

Sec. 3. And be it further enacted, That it shall not be lawful for any person or persons to bring into this state after the passage of this act, any negro or mulatto, who shall be a slave or held to service at the time, for the purpose of emancipating or setting at liberty any such negro or mulatto; and any person or persons, who shall so bring in any such negro or mulatto for the purpose aforesaid, shall give a bond to the county commissioners of the county where such slave or slaves are emancipated, in the penalty of one thousand dollars, conditioned that such person so emancipated by him, shall not become a charge on any county in this state; and every person neglecting or refusing to give such bond, shall forfeit and pay the sum of two hundred dollars for each negro or mulatto so emanicpated or set at liberty, to be recovered by action of debt before any court competent to try the same, to be sued for in the name of the county commissioners of the county, where the same shall happen, to the use of the county.

Sec. 4. And be it further enacted, That every black or mulatto person, (slaves and persons held to service excepted) residing in this state at the passage of this act, shall on or before the first day of June next, enter his or their name (unless they have heretofore entered the same,) together with the name or names of his or her family, with the clerk of the circuit court of the county in which they reside, together with the evidence of his or her freedom; which shall be entered on record by the said clerk, together with a description of all such persons; and thereafter the clerk's certificate of such record shall be sufficient evidence of his or her freedom:--Provided nevertheless, That nothing in this act contained, shall be construed to bar the lawful claim of any person or persons to any such negro or mulatto.

Sec. 5. And be it further enacted, That it shall not be lawful for any person or persons residing in this state after the first day of June next, to hire, or in any wise employ any black or mulatto person, unless such person shall have one of the certificates aforesaid; and any person who shall hire or employ any black or mulatto person contrary to the provisions of this section, shall pay the sum of one dollar and fifty-cents for each day they shall hire or employ any such; black or mulatto person, recoverable before any justice of the peace, or court competent to try the same, in the name of the county commissioners of the county where the offence may be committed; one third thereof to the person giving the information, and the other two-thirds shall be paid to the owner or owners of the black or mulatto person, if any there shall be, and apply for the same.

Sec. 6. And be it further enacted, That if any person or persons, shall harbor or secrete any black or mulatto person, the same being a slave or owing service or labor to any other person or persons, and knowing the owner or owners of such slaves or servants from retaking and possessing his or their slave or servant, shall be deemed guilty of felony, and upon conviction thereof, before any court competent to try the same, shall suffer the pains and penalties prescribed by the law for persons guilty of receiving stolen goods, knowing them to be stolen.

Sec. 7. And be it further enacted, That every black or mulatto person who shall be found in this state, and not having such a certificate as is required by this act, shall be deemed a runaway slave or servant; and it shall be lawful for any inhabitant of this, to take such black or mulatto person and carry them before some justice of the peace; and should such black or mulatto person not produce such certificate as aforesaid, it shall be the duty of such justice to cause such black or mulatto person, to be committed to the custody of the sheriff of the county, who shall keep such black or mulatto person, and in three days after receiving them, shall advertise them at the door of the court house, and shall transmit a notice and cause the same to be advertised for six weeks in some public newspaper, printed nearest to the place of apprehending such black person or mulatto, stating a description of the most remarkable features of such supposed runaway; and if such person, so committed, shall not procure a certificate or other evidence of their freedom within the time aforesaid, it shall be the duty of the sheriff to hire them out for the best price he can get, after having given five days previous notice thereof, from month to month, for the space of one year.--And if no owner shall appear and substantiate their claim before the expiration of one year, the sheriff shall give a certificate to such black or mulatto person, who on producing the same to the next circuit court of the county, may obtain a certificate from the court, stating the facts, and that the person shall be deemed a free person, unless they shall be lawfully claimed by their proper owner or owners thereafter. And as a reward to the taker up of such negro, there shall be paid by the owner, if any, before he shall receive him from the sheriff, ten dollars, and the owner shall moreover pay to the sheriff for the justice, two dollars, and reasonable costs for carrying such runaway to the sheriff; and shall also pay the sheriff all fees for keeping such runaway as other prisoners: Provided however, That the proper owner, if any there be, shall be entitled to the hire of any such runaway from the sheriff, after deducting the expenses of the same: And provided also, That the taker up shall have a right to claim any reward which the owner shall have offered for the apprehension of such runaway; should any taker up claim such offered reward, he shall not be entitled to the allowance made by this act.

Sec. 8. And be it further enacted, That in case any black or mulatto person shall not be claimed by the owner in the time aforesaid, and such person shall have obtained a certificate from the court aforesaid, they shall receive all the amount of the wages for which they may have been hired, after paying the expenses; and any person applying to the proper authority as provided by the laws of the United States, or of this state, for judging in such cases for reclaiming any black or mulatto person as his, her, or their slave or servant, and whose character for veracity, is not such as to satisfy any judge or justice of the peace, or other proper authority, that the oath or representation of such claimant is entitled to credit; and should such claimant be a stranger, it will be necessary that such authority should be made satisfied that such claimant or claimants are citizens of the United States, and that they are entitled to such credit as is before required, before they act thereon, otherwise than securing those claimed, until a decision can be had therein; and should any person or persons fraudulently obtain possession of any free negro or mulatto, by false swearing before any competent authority, such person or persons so offending, shall be deemed guilty of perjury, and on conviction thereof, shall be liable to suffer the penalties prescribed by law for such offences.

Sec. 9. And be it further enacted, That any person or persons, who shall forcibly take and carry out of this state any negro or mulatto, (slaves excepted by their owners,) owing service or labor to any person in this state, or who shall forcibly take out of this state, any free negro or mulatto having gained a legal settlement in this state, shall forfeit and pay for every such offence the sum of one thousand dollars to the party injured, to be recovered in the name of the people of the state of Illinois, by action of debt in any court having cognizance of the same: Provided however, That this section shall not be construed so as to prevent the owner or owners, or their agents, from removing their servants, who shall runaway and be found in this state, to any state or territory where they may belong, nor to persons who shall be travelling or removing their servants through this state, to any other state or territory.

Sec. 10. And be it further enacted, That servants shall be provided by the master with wholesome and sufficient food, clothing, and lodging, and at the end of their service, if they shall not have contracted for any reward, food, clothing and lodging, shall receive from him one new and complete suit of clothing suited to the season of the year, to-wit: a coat, waist coat, pair of breeches, and shoes, two pair of stockings, two shirts, a hat and blanket.

Sec. 11. And be it further enacted, That the benefit of the said contract of service, shall be assignable by the master to any person being a citizen of this state, to whom the servant shall in the presence of a justice of the peace, freely consent, that it shall be assigned; the said justice, attesting such free consent in writing; and shall also pass to the executors, administrators and legatees of the master.

Sec. 12. And be it further enacted, That any such servant being lazy, disorderly, guilty of misbehavior to his master, or master's family, shall be corrected by stripes, on order from a justice of the county, wherein he resides; or refusing to work, shall be compelled thereto in like manner, and moreover shall serve two days for every one he shall have so refused to serve, or shall otherwise have lost, without sufficient justification; all necessary expences incurred by any master for apprehending and bringing home any obsconding servant, shall be repaid by further services, after such rates as the circuit court of the county shall direct, unless such

8

servant shall give security, to be approved of
by the court for the payment in money within six
months after he shall be free from service, and
shall accordingly pay the same.

Sec. 13. And be it further enacted, That if
any master shall fail in the duties prescribed
by this act, or shall be guilty of injurious
demeanor towards his servant, it shall be redre-
ssed on motion, by the circuit court of the
county wherein the servant resides, who may hear
and determine such cases in a summary way, making such orders thereupon, as in their judgment
will relieve the party injured in future.

Sec. 14. And be it further enacted, That all
contracts between masters and servants, during
the time of service, shall be void.

Sec. 15. And be it further enacted, That the
circuit court of every county shall, at all
times, receive the complaints of servants, being
citizens of any of the United States of America,
who reside within the jurisdiction of such
court, against their masters or mistresses,
alledging undeserved or immoderate correction,
insufficent allowances of food, raiment, or
lodging, and may hear and determine such case in
a summary way, making such orders thereupon as
in their judgment will relieve the party injured
in future; and may also, in the same manner hear
and determine complaints of masters and mistresses against their servants, for desertion without good cause, and may oblige the latter for
loss thereby occasioned, to make restitution by
futher services after the expiration of the
time, for which they had been bound.

Sec. 16. And be it futher enacted, That if
any servant shall at any time bring in goods or
money, during time of their service, shall by
gift, or other lawful means, acquire goods or
money, they shall have the property, and benefit
thereof, to their own use; and if any servant
shall be sick or lame, and so become useless or
chargeable, his or her master or owner, shall
maintain such servant, until his or her time of
service shall be expired; and if any master or
owner, shall put away any lame or sick servant,
under pretence of freedom, and such servant bec-

omes chargeable to the county, such master or owner, shall forfeit and pay thirty dollars, to the overseers of the poor of the county, wherein such offence shall be committed, to the use of the poor of the county, recoverable with costs, by action of debt in any circuit court; and moreover, shall be liable to the action of the said overseers of the poor at the common law for damages.

Sec. 17. And be it further enacted, That no negro, mulatto, or indian, shall at any time purchase any servant, other than of their own complexion, and if any of the persons aforesaid, shall nevertheless presume to purchase a white servant, such servant shall immediately become free, and shall be so held, deemed and taken.

Sec. 18. And be it further enacted, That no person shall buy, sell or receive of, to, or from any servant or slave any coin or commodity without leave or consent of the master or owner of such slave or servant; and any person so offending shall forfeit and pay to the master or owner of such slave or servant four times the valaue of the thing so bought, sold or recovered, to be recovered with costs of suit before any court having cognizance of the same; and every servant upon the expiration of his or her time shall be entitled to a certificate from the clerk of the court of the county where such servant is indentured or registered, and such certificate shall indemnify any person for hiring or employing such person.

Sec. 19. And be it further enacted, That in all cases of penal laws where free persons are punishable by fine, servants shall be punished by whipping, after the rate of twenty lashes for every eight dollars, so that no servant shall receive more than forty lashes at any one time, unless such offender can procure some person to pay the fine.

Sec. 20. And be it further enacted, That every servant upon the expiration of his or her time, and proof thereof made before the circuit court of the county, where he or she last served, shall have his or her freedom recorded and a certificate thereof, under the hand of the clerk, which shall be sufficient to indemnify any person for entertaining or hiring such servant; and if such certificate should happen to be torn or lost, the clerk, upon request shall issue another, reciting therein the loss of the former.

Sec. 21. And be it further enacted, That if any slave or servant shall be found at a distance of ten miles from the tenement of his or her master, or the person with whom he or she lives, without a pass or some letter of token, whereby it may appear that he or she is proceeding by authority from his or her master, employer or overseer, it shall and may be lawful for any person to apprehend and carry him or her before a justice of the peace, to be by his order punished with stripes, not exceeding thirty-five, at his discretion.

Sec. 22. And be it further enacted, That if any slave or servant shall presume to come and be upon the plantation, or the dwelling of any person whatsover, without leave from his or her owner, not being sent upon lawful business, it shall be lawful for the owner of such plantation, or dwelling house to give or order such slave or servant, ten lashes on his or her bare back.

Sec. 23. And be it further enacted, That riots, routs, unlawful assemblies, trespasses and seditious speeches, by any slave or slaves, servant or servants, shall be punished with stripes, at the discretion of a justice of the peace, not exceeding thirty-nine, and he who will, may apprehend and carry him, her or them before such justice.

Sec. 24. And be it further enacted, That if any person or persons shall permit or suffer any slave or slaves, servant or servants of color, to the number of three or more, to assemble in his, her or their house, out house, yard or shed for the purpose of dancing or revelling, either by night or by day, the person or persons so offending shall forfeit and pay the sum of twenty dollars, with costs, to any person or persons who will sue for and recover the same, by action of debt or indictment, in any court of record proper to try the same.

Sec. 25. And be it further enacted, That it shall be the duty of all coroners, sheriffs, judges and justices of the peace, who shall see or known of, or be informed of any such assemblage of slaves or servants, immediately to commit such slaves or servants to the jail of the county; and on view or proof thereof, order each and every such slave or servant to be whipped, not exceeding thirty-nine stripes, on his or her bare back, on the day next succeeding such assemblage, unless it shall happen on a Sunday, then on the Monday following; which said stripes shall be inflicted by any constable of the township, if there should be one therein, or otherwise by any person or persons whom the said justices shall appoint, and who shall be willing so to inflict the same:--Provided however, That the provisions hereof shall not apply to any persons of color, who may assemble for the purpose of amusement, by permission of their masters first had in writing, on condition that no disorderly conduct is made use of by them in such assemblage. Approved, March 30, 1819." (Perrin 158-169)

Specifically, section six of the preceding code was clarified in the Illinois criminal code.

"...every such person so offending shall be deemed guilty of a misdemeanor, and fined not exceeding $500 or imprisoned not exceeding six months."(Hand 46)

"...Thus was the free state of Illinois provided with a complete slave code." (Davidson 318)

Provisions were also passed by the state of Illinois restricting negroes from permanently settling within its borders. Article XIV of the Constitution of 1848 stipulated that:

"The general assembly shall, at its first session under the amended constitution, pass such laws as will effectually prohibit free persons of color from immigrating to and settling in this state; and to effectually prevent owners of slaves from bringing them into this state for the purpose of setting them free." (Moses 110)

18

Apparently, such a provision, still needed re-enforcement because another statute was created in 1853 that provided:

"If any person or persons shall bring, or cause to be brought into this state, any negro or mulatto slave, whether said slave is set free or not, (he) shall be liable to an indictment, and, upon conviction thereof, be fined for every such negro or mulatto, a sum not less than one hundred dollars, nor more than five hundred dollars, and imprisoned in the county jail not more than one year, and shall stand committed until said fine and costs are paid." (Gertz 466)

Even during the Civil War, the state general assembly still passed statutes emulating the man of color within their boundaries. In the proposed constitution of 1862, summarily rejected by the citizens at the polls, it contained Article XVIII which read:

"Sec. 1. No negro or mulatto shall migrate to or settle in this state, after the adoption of this constitution.

Sec. 2. No negro or mulatto shall have the right of suffrage, or hold any office in this state.

Sec. 3. The general assembly shall pass all laws necessary to carry into effect the provisions of this article."(Gertz 467)

In the next year on 1 January 1863, Abraham Lincoln as the President of the United States, issued a proclamation stating:

"That on the first day of January, in the year of our Lord 1863, all persons held as slaves within any state or designated part of a state, the people whereof shall then be in rebellion against the United States, shall be then, henceforward, and forever free; and the Executive Government of the United States, including the military and naval authority thereof, will recognize and maintain the freedom of such persons, or any of them, in any efforts they may make for their actual freedom."(Lincoln Vol VI 29)

It was almost a year later, 11 January 1864, that a joint resolution which proposed an amendment to the Constitution forever prohibiting slavery in the States and territories was amended and passed by the Senate on April 11. However, the House failed to receive the necessary two-thirds majority until January 31, 1865. The ressolution and amendment were approved by Abraham Lincoln, February 1, 1865, and adopted by the requisite three-fourths of the states and became the Thirteenth Amendment to the Constitution. (Lincoln Vol VI 29)

The state of Illinois repealed all the laws concerning the negroes and mulattoes on February 7th that same year. Thus from 1819 to 1865,...

"efforts were repeatedly made to abolish them (the laws). But they had ceased to be enforced for many years previously, and, except the act of 1853, were regarded as a dead letter. The obstinacy with which they were retained was owing in great part to the Abolition excitement of modern times, which in a manner constituted them tests of party fealty." (Davidson 328)

Illinois thus became treacherous ground for runaways as evidenced by contemporary runaway and sheriff notices placed in various Illinois newspapers. As required by statute, the owner or person in authority gave a physical description of the runaway; in contrast, the notices placed in southern newspapers rarely included a physical description.

One undeniable fact that surfaced from these notices was indeed the Tennessee and Cumberland Rivers were an avenue of "all roads leading to Rome" for the fugitive slave.

RUN away, on the 3d Day of *May* last, a young Negro Boy, named *Joe*, this Country born, formerly belonged to Capt. *Hugh Hext*. Whoever brings the said Boy the Subscriber at *Edisto* or to the Work House in *Charles Town*, shall have 3 *l* reward On the contrary whoever harbours the said Boy, may depend upon being severely prosecuted, by

Thomas *Chisam*.

WALTER DUNBAR, Per-

ADVERTISEMENT FOR A RUN-AWAY SLAVE

ILLINOIS GAZETTE, Shawneetown, Ill., 27 November 1819
    Run away from the subscriber, living in Cal-
dwell County, Kentucky, eight miles north of Eddyville, on or about the 15th October, Eda, a bright
mulatto woman, about 26 years of age, common height,
a scar on the right side of her forehead, and one on
her neck, had on when she went away, a yellow groun-
ded linsey dress, and took with her a cotton cloak.
She is a very likely wench, wears her hair straight-
combed and tied, talks fluently, except when closely
questioned, when she stammers and appears much embar-
rassed.
    The above reward will be given to any person
who will deliver her to me, at my residence, to Mr.
Geo. W. Frazer, eight miles below Shawneetown, on the
Ohio.
Vincent Anderson, Shawneetown, Nov. 27, 1819

ILLINOIS GAZETTE, Shawneetown, Ill., 27 January 1820
    Ran away from the subscriber, living on the
waters of Piney Creek, in Livingston County, Kentucky, on the night of the 15th instant, a tall Negro
man, named Moses, about 28 years old, marked with a
few gray hairs on his head, round faced, very long
feet, long slim fingers, and about six feet height.
Had on, when he went away, a roundabout coat, blue
cloth overalls, a wool hat, with red ?, very little
worn. Took with him, among other articles, two blankets. He undoubtedly came in to Illinois, but whether
he will remain there or go across the Wabash or
Mississippi, is not conjectured.
    Any person who will deliver him to Flinn's or
Frazer's Ferry -- or confine him in Shawneetown Jail,
and give me notice thereof, -- shall have the above
reward.
Elisha Thurmand, Shawneetown, Dec. 20, 1819

ILLINOIS GAZETTE, Shawneetown, Ill., 3 February 1820
    On the 8th instant, to the jail in this place,
a negro man named Dave, about 6 feet high, 19 to 20
yeares old, well built, dark complexion, is dressed

in homemade linsey, with the exception of an old blue great coat.

Says he belongs to Archibald White, ten miles from Huntsville, Alabama

The owner is requested to prove him, pay charges, and take him away.

M.S. Davenport, Sheriff, Gallatin County, Ill. Shawneetown, 11 January 1820

ILLINOIS GAZETTE, Shawneetown, Ill., 17 February 1820

Ran away from the subscriber on the night of 9th instant, a Negro man named Buck, a light mulatto, about 22 years of age, 5 feet 11 inches or 6 feet high, straight and well made, but rather slender, has a down cast look when spoken to, as he had a variety of clothing, is difficult to describe them. He has been accustomed to work in a tabacco manufactory, and is a good rough shoemaker. Being an artful cunning fellow, he may procure forged papers and attempt to pass for a free man.

The above reward will be given to his delivery here, to N. & J. Dick & Co., New Orleans, or for securing him in jail so that get him again.

George Atkinson, Henderson, Kentucky, 14 Feb. 1820

ILLINOIS GAZETTE. Shawneetown, Ill., 24 February 1820

Ran away from the U.S. Saline, Ill. on the 14th instant, a Negro man, named Dick, 5 feet 9 inches high, stoutly made, 22 or 23 years old, and very black and ugly. He has a small scar on his forehead, cut with a knife, and one on his left breast. His feet singularly shaped, being very narrow at the heel and broad at the toes, his eyes generally red. He is fond of spirits, and will steal anything upon which he can lay his hands.

He is the same fellow that absconded from Mr. David Garnsey of Missouri last July, and who put in Herculaneum Jail for attempting to commit a rape upon a white woman. From some circumstances, I am disposed to think that he will go down the river, but whether he will endeavor to get in Texas, or stop in any of the states or turn ones bordering on the Mississippi is doubtful.

Any person taking up said negro within this state shall receive a reward of fifty dollars, and if

16

taken anywhere out of the state, and notice given me, thereof, so that I obtain possession of him again, a reward of one hundred dollars, and all reasonable charges for bringing him to me.

John Forrester, Shawneetown, IL, 20 Feb. 1819

ILLINOIS GAZETTE, Shawneetown, Ill., 24 February 1820

Run away from my farm in Logan County, Kentucky, on July last, a negro man, by the name of Jacob. He is a low, chunky made fellow not five feet high, coal black, a large scar on the side of his face in the edge of his hair, occasioned by a burn, 23 years old.

Any person delivering said negro to me shall have the above reward, and all resasonable charges paid.

Elisha Prince

ILLINOIS GAZETTE, Shawneetown, Ill., 2 March 1820

Ran away from the subscriber, some time about the first of January last, from the United States Saline, hired to Timothy Gard, Esq., a negro man named Jacob, very black, about 38 years of age, five feet four or five inches high, chunky for his height; somewhat inclined to be bowlegged, has a fierce look when spoken to. As he had been at work at the Lick, it is difficult to describe his clothing. He has been accostomed to a variety of work such as on a farm, on the river, at the Lick, etc. Being an artful cunning fellow, he may procure forged papers, and attempt to pass as a free man, perhaps may call his name Jacob Herral. The above reward will be given for the delivering of him to the subscribers, Morgantown, Kentucky, or to Timothy Gard, Esq., United States Saline, or for securing him in jail so that I get him again.

James A. Porter & Co., Shawneetown, March 2, 1820.

ILLINOIS GAZETTE, Shawneetown, Ill., 10 June 1820

There are two negro fellows, runaways, now in confinement, in the jail of White County, State of Illinois, who call their names Harry and Anderson. Henry has a club fist, which he says, was occasioned by a burn when young; says he belongs to Allen Morris of Franklin Co., Tenn. Anderson says he belongs to James McDaniel of Limestone County, Ala.

Daniel Hay, Sheriff of White Co., 29 May 1820

ILLINOIS GAZETTE, Shawneetown, Ill., 8 July 1820
Ranaway from the subscriber's plantation in
Franklin County, state of Alabama, near Florence, on
the 7th of this month, three negroes, Charles and his
wife Melberry, and Sam. Charles is about 5 feet eight
or ten inches high, 36 or 37 years old; was raised
near the Falls of Tar River, in the state of North
Carolina; is very sensible; has but one eye, and, I
am told, can write, and may have procurred a pass for
all three. He has a quantity of clothing, among which
is a blue coarse surfcut coat, a blue stripe waistcoat, a pair of shoe-boots, a pair of coarse tow
cloth pantaloons, and shirt. He is a coarse carpenter, and can saw very well with the whip-saw.
Melberry, the wife of Charles, is of common
size, 28 or 29 years of age, has a variety of clothing with her, several dresses of calico and white
cambrick. She is a sickly woman, and has a yellowish
complexion.
Sam is low and chunky, very thick lips, with a
down look, about 36 years of age, his clothing is not
remembered, except a brown coat of very coarse coa-
ting, which fits him badly. He has a rupture in the
lower part of his abdomen, and commonly wears a belt.
All of them, I expect, are free from marks of
the whip, as neither of them has ever been stricken
since I owned them, which is about five years. It is
supposed they were carried off by some white men, and
that they will aim for the state of Illinois, Indiana
or Ohio, or go back to the county of Edgecombe, in
North Carolina.
The above reward will be given for securing
them in any gaol out of this state, a liberal reward
will be paid if taken in this state.
Theo. W. Cockburn, Florence, Ala. 12 June 1820

ILLINOIS GAZETTE, Shawneetown, Ill. 12 August 1820
Ranaway from the subscriber, living at Cumberland Furnace, Dickson Co., Tenn. the following negroes, viz. Bob, a negro man, about 25 or 28 years
old, five feet seven or eight inches high, round
shouldered, full negro but not deep black--his two
middle toes on each foot contracted. He made his
escape some time in September 1819. Isham and Dick

18

ran away from my boat as it ascended the Mississippi on the 25th of June last, about twenty miles below Kaskaskia. Isham is a mulatto, about 24 or 25 years old, about 5 feet 8 or 9 inches high, a likely well formed intelligent fellow, his feet tolerable large and fleshy. Dick, a black negro, about 25 or 26 years old, about five feet seven or eight inches high, active and well formed, no particular flesh mark recollected. Tom and Tobias, runaways from this place on the 30th of June. Tom is a very bright mulatto, almost white, but his hair has perceivably the curl of a negro--he is about 20 or 21 years old, about 5 feet 8 or 9 inches high, straight well-formed likely fellow and very intelligent, has been accustomed to moulding, but handles tools pretty well as a rough carpenter. The negro can be perceived by his nose and hair, his nose being shorter, larger and flatter than those of white men generally. Tobias, a mulatto about 5 feet 7 or 8 inches high, about 28 or 29 years old, slender form, carrying but little flesh, much marked with the whip, his feet long and slender for a negro. Their clothing not recollected except Tom--he took with him a fashionable made blue broad cloth boat but may have changed it. Those negroes may, or may not, have forged a certificate of their citizenship, either written or printed--I will give the above reward, for either or all of the above negroes, if lodged in any jail and securely ironed so that I get them, or will pay reasonable expenses if brought home. Any persons apprehending these negroes must securely iron them, or they will make their escape. It is supposed they will bend their course towards the free states.

Montgomery Bell, Clarksville, 7 July 1820

ILLINOIS GAZETTE, Shawneetown, Ill. 30 September 1820

Ran away from the subscribers, living in Warren County, Kentucky, on the night of the 17th inst. five negro men and one woman. Viz. Peter, 23 years old, 5 feet 10 inches high, thick lips, broad flat feet, black complexion. Another of the same name, a bright mulatto, 22 years old, 5 feet 9 or 10 inches high, heavy well made, very active, black complexion. Randle, a bright mulatto, 19 years old, 5 feet 9 inches high and blue eyes. Goan, 20 years old, black complexion, 5 feet 10 inches high. And a girl, named Sal, 22 years old, yellow complexion. The above reward will be given to any person, on apprehending said negroes and confining them in any jail, so that we get them or $25 to secure either of them and we will pay all reasonable charges. Any person, taking up all or either of said negroes, will give information to Samuel S. Brooking, Bowling Green, Kentucky.

Leroy Jackson, David Reid, Martin Sisk and John Stone. Sept. 24th, 1820

ILLINOIS GAZETTE, Shawneetown, Ill. 30 September 1820

Ran away from the subscriber, living in the parish of Pelican, Louisiana, on the 28th of May last, a negro man, named Bob--he is 23 or 24 years old, 6 feet or upwards high, has a very black complexion, bad countenance, uncommon large mouth, large red eyes, small piece taken out of one of his ears, long legs, large feet with long heels. Bob was taken up and put in Salem jail, Ky., but has made his escape from it since--and is now supposed to be making for some of the freee states.

Any person, taking up and securing, said Bob, in some jail, so that I get him again, shall receive the above reward--and if brought to the subscriber, all reasonable charges shall be paid.

John McKneely, Sept. 25th, 1820

ILLINOIS GAZETTE, Shawneetown, Ill. 14 October 1820

Runaway slaves or servants. Taken up and now in Pope County jail, two black men and one black woman, supposed to be runaway slaves or servants. They call their names Dennis, James and Betsey.

Dennis about 28 years of age, has a scar over his left eyebrow, fingers and thumb of the right hand burnt off to the first joint--about 5 feet 6 inches high, tolerably round featured, forehead a little projecting, thin lips, says he has been married to the black woman for two years.

James is about 30 years of age, and short thick set, about 5 feet high, short wool on his breast and small whiskers--has a small scar on his left shoulder caused by a fall from a horse as he says while a rider for Mr. Gassway of Alexandria, D.C.

Betsey says she has been married to Dennis for two years. She is about 15 years of age, about 5 feet high, flat nose, has no marks or scars.

The two men say that, while young, they, with

30 or 40 slaves, were set free at the death of their master, Charles Carter, counsellor at law, lower part of Fairfax County, Va. but continued to reside in the family until they were about 18 years of age,--and that Betsey's mother belonged to the same family, and was liberated at the same time. She was born several years after when they were first apprehended. They said they belonged to Robert Farren at or near the Chickasaw Bluffs.

If certificates of freedom are not produced before the expiration of six weeks publication of this advertisement, or the owner or owners do not appear, and substantiate their claim, as the law requires, within one year, they will be farmed out, and disposed of according to the laws of this state. Dated Golconda, Pope County, Oct. 3, 1820. Amos Chipps, Sheriff Pope County, Ill. Oct. 13, 1820

ILLINOIS GAZETTE, Shawneetown, Ill. 2 December 1820

Ran away from the subscriber, living in Livingston County, near Salem, Kentucky, about the 20th of the present inst., a mulatto man, about 23 years of age, about 6 feet high, trim well made fellow, down look when spoken to; he has the mark of a burn on his belly, and one of his knees, his name is Jake, may call himself Jacob Breckenridge, he wore a blue broad cloth coat, and took a drab great coat with him. The above reward, with all reasonable expenses, will be paid if brought home.

William Thomson, 27 Nov. 1820

ILLINOIS GAZETTE, Shawneetown, Ill. 10 March 1821

Ran away on the 4th of April last, from the subscriber, living in Davidson County, near Nashville, Tenn., one negro man named Parmer, supposed to have left the neighborhood of Nashville about the 18th of Nov. 1820. This negro is supposed to have attempted to cross the Ohio near Shawneetown, Ill. He is about 5 feet 6 or 7 inches high, well made, about 26 or 27 years of age, yellowish cast, has a very pleasing countenance; large flat feet with wonderful large cracks in his heels, rather inclined to be bow legged, very large hands, an upper tooth out before, very short wool on his head, and has considerable assurance in conversation. The above reward will be given to any person apprehending and delivering said

negro to me, or $20, if secured in any jail in either
of the states of Ohio, Indiana, Illinois or Kentucky,
so I get him again.

William Murphey, Dec. 20, 1820

ILLINOIS GAZETTE, Shawneetown, Ill. 10 March 1821

Ran away from the subscriber, living in Davidson County, below Nashville, Tenn. about the 18th
Nov. last, a small negro man named Merit, about 18 or
20 years of age, about 5 feet 4 or 5 inches high,
stout build, bow legged, round head and face. This
negro is supposed to have runaway in company with
William Murphey's from Tennessee. He is supposed to
have aimed for Illinois state, and probably crossed
about Shawneetown. I will give $20 to any person
securing said negro in any jail in the state of
Illinois, Indiana, Ohio or Kentucky, so I get him
again or $50 if delivered to me, living seven miles
below Nashville, Tenn.

James H. Williams, 20 Dec. 1820. The printer of
the Western Sun, Vincennes, will please give the two
foregoing advertisements four insertions successively
in his paper, and forward his account to Nashville,
Tenn. for payment.

ILLINOIS GAZETTE, Shawneetown, Ill. 24 March 1821

Ran away from the subscriber, living 18 miles
from Florence, Lauderdale County, a negro fellow
named Jack, rather of a yellow complexion, about 5
feet 9 or 10 inches high, tolerably stout made, slow
spoken, diffident in his manners, has a wide gap in
his upper foreteeth and would be supposed that he had
lost one of them; he had on him a pale blue superfine
broadcloth coat, much worn, a fur hat--his other
clothing cannot be described. Whoever will take up
said negro and deliver him in Florence shall receive
$25, and all reasonable expenses paid, and if secured
out of the state so that I get him, $50.

Thomas Crittenden. The editors of the Shawneetown paper and Spectator, Edwardsville, Ill. will
give the above three insertions and send their accounts to this office for payment. 8 March 1821

ILLINOIS GAZETTE, Shawneetown, Ill. 24 March 1821

Ran away from the subscriber, on the night of
the 12th inst., a negro man named Ben--about 35 years

22

of age, about 5 feet 10 inches high, lofty carriage, and when in motion, one of his knees bends in more than the other, rather of a yellow complexion. Carried away with him two surcut coats, one green, the other blue, nearly worn out, a fur hat about half worn, two blankets, one pair of shoes, and one pair of Monroe shoes--also, he had two coarse linen shirts new. I think it probable he will aim for the English Prairie or Vincennes. The above reward will be given to any person who will deliver said negro to me, living in Carmi, Illinois, or $15, if confined in any jail in this state, and information given me so that I get him.

William P. Richardson, Carmi. 13 Feb. 1821

ILLINOIS GAZETTE, Shawneetown, 14 April 1821

Was committed to the jail in Pope County, there being none in Gallatin County, on the 12th of March last, a negro man, named Charles, about 5 feet 7 or 8 inches high, apparently 26 or 27 years of age, dark colour, rather a thin visage--He says that he has been free about three years, and is from Robeson County, Tenn. He had a pass (supposed to be forged), which is signed George Strother, who probably is his real master. Now, if the said supposed runaway shall not be claimed within the space of six weeks from this date, he will be hired out, as the law directs, for the term of one year.

Richard T. Jones, Sheriff of Gallatin County, Ill. Shawneetown, 14 April 1821

ILLINOIS GAZETTE, Shawneetown, Ill. 12 May 1821

I will give the above reward of one hundred dollars, in silver, if required, to any person who will apprehend and bring me my mulatto man, Jerry, or $50, if secured in any jail of any distant state so that I get him. Jerry has a piece bit off one ear, is of common stature, about 40 years old, a very bright ? mulatto, straight black hair, and looks like an Indian. I expect he will try to pass for a Chickasaw, as there was one of that tribe, calling himself John Underwood, who left my home a few days before said runaway started. Jerry is a very good hewer and tolerable carpenter--I expect he will follow said employment. The United States Agents in the Cherokee and Chickasaw nations, would oblige me by inquiring of the people, over whom they preside, concerning him, and should they discover said slave, to write to me at Hendersonville, P.O. in Newbury District, South Carolina, where I will respond for any favours as above required, according as promise.

   Lewis Hogg, 12th May 1821

ILLINOIS GAZETTE, Shawneetown, Ill. 16 June 1821

  Ran away from the subscribers on the night of the 21st of April, the following negroes, to wit: Tom, a likely yellow fellow, about 22 years old, near 6 feet high, can read and write; Abram, a thick heavy made black fellow, about 28 years old, has a large mouth with very large thick lips, large eyes, his ankles are apt to swell; Harry, a likely black fellow, about 23 years old, near 6 feet high, had, when he left home, some very good clothing. Hubbard, a black fellow, about 25 years old, 5 feet 6 or 8 inches high, well made--the above reward will be given for committing said negroes in any jail, so that we get them, or 50 dollars for any one of them; the yellow man Tom had a gun and a watch, which he took with him. N.B. Communications relative to the above negroes, will please be made to James W. Camp, Elkton, state of Tennessee.

   James W. Camp, Jesse Penn, Aaron Brown, John N. Smith. Elkton, June 9, 1821

ILLINOIS GAZETTE, Shawneetown, Ill. 30 June 1821

  $35 reward will be given for the apprehending and confining in any jail, so that I get him again, a negro man named Bill--very light complexion, and a down look--had on when he went off a handcuff on the left wrist, dark woolen roundabout, dark gray cassimere pantaloons, he is about 5 feet 8 or 10 inches high, 21 or 22 years of age--or I will give $50 to any person who will confine him on board any steam boat and deliver him to me at Natchez. If confined in jail, write to me at Bardstown, Ky.--the boy left me at this place today.

   William Cotton, Smithland, Ky. 21 June 1821

ILLINOIS GAZETTE, Shawneetown, Ill. 7 July 1821

  Taken up, a negro man, who calls himself John and who states he is the property of Mr. James Hannan, a citizen of the Alabama Territory. The said negro has had his left thigh broken and walks with a half, about 25 years old. He has been secreted on the opposite side of the Ohio, near the mouth of the Tennessee River, but is now in my possession for the benefit of the owner.

J.D. Wilcox, Fort Massac, Ill. 25 June 1821

ILLINOIS GAZETTE, Shawneetown, Ill. 7 July 1821

Was committed to the jail of Pope County, state of Illinois, a negro man by the name of Lewis, about 23 years of age, black colour, thick lips, long foreteeth, and one of them missing. About 5 feet 6 inches high, a native of Africa. He says his master is by the name of James Wright, living on Elk River, about 45 miles above Fayettesville, near to Hall's Mill, Tenn.

Amos Chipps, Sheriff of Pope Co. 7 July 1821

ILLINOIS GAZETTE, Shawneetown, Ill. 21 July 1821

Ran away from my plantation, near Florence, Alabama, on the night of the 18th inst. two negro men and one woman--Peter, Harry and Cate. Peter is a very stout likely fellow, not very black, rather high cheek bones, fleshy in the face, speaks loud, supposed to be 25 years old; his clothing was a white cotton shirt and pantaloons. Harry is of common size, well made, very black, pert and active, from 25 to 30 years of age; had on when he left home, a white cotton shirt and pantaloons. Cate is a little under the common size, very black, likely and well made, speaks lively; took with her one or two striped cotton coats; about 24 or 25 years of age. They stole a sorrel horse, 14 1/2 hands high.

They were all brought from North Carolina, where they endeavour to return, or make their way to Illinois, Indiana or Ohio. If they attempt to get across the Ohio, they will most probably be conducted by a notorious scoundral called Willis, who lately belonged to Peter R. Booker of Columbia, and still may be his property who went off from my neighborhood about the same time. He was charged with housebreaking in Columbia, and severely beat a white man near that place, for which he was apprehended, but by some means was gotten out of the hands of justice. Willis is about 6 feet high, very likely, yellow complexion, and stout made. Any person securing the above negroes so that I get them, shall have the above reward if taken out of state, or half the amount offered if taken in Alabama, and all expenses paid or for any one of them in like proportion.

James Jackson, 14th July 1821. The Register, Knoxville, and Republican, Huntsville, are requested to publish the above advertisement six times and forward their accounts to Florence, Alabama.

ILLINOIS GAZETTE, Shawneetown, Ill. 4 August 1821

Ran away yesterday afternoon, a negro man named Tom, about 18 or 19 years old, 5 feet 2 or 3 inches high, well built, dark colour with a large flat nose, down look but rather cunning. Had on a plaid roundabout, brown linen pantaloons, and an old fur hat. Took with him a good blue cloth coat, a pair of domestic pantaloons and several other articles of clothing. It is expected that he has taken a horse with him. He was seen on Saturday last conversing with a French boy from Vincennes, and it is quite likely he has accompanied him to that place, as he was raised somewhere in that quarter. I will give $25 to any person taking him in this state or $35 if taken out of this state, and secured so that I get him.

Moses M. Rawlings, Shawneetown, Ill. 30 July 1821

ILLINOIS GAZETTE, Shawneetown, Ill. 23 August 1821

Ran away from the Paragon steam boat, on Tuesday, the 31st of July, a negro man by the name of Fred, about 50 years of age, about 5 feet 7 inches high, stout build, had on when he ran from the boat, white shirt and trousers; he took down the river, and will probably make his way towards Morganfield or Shawneetown. The above reward will be given, and all reasonable charges allowed on his being delivered to the subscriber, at his store in Henderson, or secured in any jail where the rightful owner may obtain his property.

Caleb Fellows, Henderson. Aug. 1, 1821

ILLINOIS GAZETTE, Shawneetown, Ill. 23 Aug. 1821

Notice, a mulatto man, who calls his name Levi Morgan, has been apprehended as a runaway, and committed to my custody, and is now in confinement in the

White County jail, state of Illinois. He is probably
45 or 50 years of age, 5 feet 8 or 9 inches high,
bald headed.
    Daniel Hay, Sheriff of White County. Aug. 6,
1821

ILLINOIS GAZETTE, Shawneetown, Ill. 17 Nov. 1821
    Ran away from the subscriber, living in Overton
County, West Tennessee, on the 17th day of July last,
a mulatto slave named Elijah, about 30 years of age,
near 6 feet high, low forehead, crooked nose and well
made, a house carpenter by trade. Had on a nearly new
smooth fur hat, his other clothing not known. It is
expected he will make for Illinois somewhere, perhaps
Vandalia. Any person apprehending and securing said
fellow so that I get him, shall have a $20 for so
doing. Give information to W. Chitton, Jr. Overton
County, W. Tennessee.
    W. Chitton, Jr. Sept. 22, 1821

ILLINOIS GAZETTE, Shawneetown, Ill. Nov. 17, 1821
    Ran away from the plantation of the subscriber,
on the 25th September last, a negro man named Rows;
27 or 28 years of age, about 6 feet high, very black,
his visage thin, eyes small, and smiles when he
speaks, his voice resembles that of a woman, his
clothing, when he went away, was plain homespun, and
much worn; it is likely that he may have supplied
himself by theft.
    The above reward of $20 will be given for his
apprehension if taken out of the state, or $10 if
taken within the state, and pay all reasonable charges for delivering him to me, living on the road from
Centreville to Eddyville, Caldwell County, Kentucky,
or securing him in jail so that I get him again.
    Henry Machen. Oct. 15, 1821

ILLINOIS GAZETTE, Shawneetown, Ill. Dec. 8, 1821
    Ran away from the subscriber, living in Montgo-
mery County, Tennessee, a negro man, named Sam, about
23 years old, weighs about 140 lbs., 5 feet 8 or 10
inches high, yellow complexion--has a blue speck in
his upper foreteeth--is a keen, well-spoken fellow,
He was in Shawneetown about a fortnight since, and
passed by the name of John. --the above reward will
be given to any person who will deliver the said neg-

ro in any jail in Kentucky or Tennessee.

Edwin Clifton. The Vincennes Sun will please publish the above, and send the account to E. Clifton. Dec. 8, 1821

ILLINOIS GAZETTE, Shawneetown, Ill. Dec. 8, 1821

Ran away, from on board the steam boat Kentucky, at Shippingport, Kentucky, on the 10th September last, a negro man named Bob, about 27 years old, and very black, 5 feet 6 inches high; has a small scar above one of his eyes, high cheek bones, and his back much scarred with the cowhide; has a down look when spoken to. He had on, when he went away, a tarpaulin hat. I will give the above reward out of the state or $100 in the state of Kentucky, and delivered to me on board the steamboat Kentucky or to J.H. Bland at Lewisville.

C. Bosworth. N.B. I was told today, that the same boy was at the Saline Salt work, tending fires. Dec. 8, 1821

ILLINOIS GAZETTE, Shawneetown, Ill. Dec. 22, 1821

$100 reward for apprehending and bringing home, Ned and Hannah, who eloped some time in August last; it is supposed they will aim to cross the Ohio, to some of the free states. Ned is a stout made, clumsey fellow, yellow complexion, about 5 feet 7 or 8 inches high, remarkable large head and face, walks with his toes out. Hannah is a small woman, 30 years of age, a squinting look out of her eyes, a remarkable scar on the upper edge of her forehead. The above reward will be given for Ned and Hannah, if brought home to the subscribers living in Todd County, Kentucky, if taken out of the state, or $50 for either of them, or $20 if secured in any jail, so that we can get them again.

W. Harlan. Thos. Jeffries. Editors of the Illinois Intelligencer and Illinois Gazette, are requested to publish the above three weeks, and forward their accounts to this office for payment. Hopkinsville, Ky. Oct. 12, 1821

ILLINOIS GAZETTE, Shawneetown, Ill. Jan. 19, 1822

Ran away from the subscriber, living in the county of Cape Girardeau, state of Missouri, two negro men, one by the name of Sampson; about 29 years of age; 6 feet high and well proportioned; he is a very black negro, thick lips, and a very pleasant, smooth talking fellow. The other named Jerry; about 25 years of age; 5 feet 5 inches high, rather slender build, a very high forehead, and I believe he has an old scar over his right eye; they both have considerable coarse cotton clothing and good great coats. Any person that will apprehend and secure said negroes, so that I get them again, shall have the above reward, and all reasonable expenses paid if brought to me.

Dec. 22, Thompson Bird. The editor of the Illinois Gazette, Shawneetown, will insert the above four weeks and forward his account to this office for payment. Jackson, Miss.

ILLINOIS GAZETTE, Shawneetown, Ill. Feb. 23, 1822

$50 reward. The above reward will paid for the apprehension and delivery to the subscriber, near Huntsville, Alabama, of a negro woman, named Peggy, about 22 years of age, full face, large eyes, black complexion, stout built, but not tall--said negro girl ran away from this place in the month of Feb. last, was apprehended at Smithland, near the mouth of the Cumberland and was brought within a few miles of this place, in the month of July or Aug. last, when she made her escape, and has not been heard from since. She attempted to pass as a free woman, and I expect she will now endeavor to reach some of the states north of the Ohio. Said woman belongs to Doctor Robert H. Rose, and when she made her first escape, was hired to Samuel K. M'Graw, of Huntsville. $20 will be paid for apprehending and committing her to any gaol in the United States so that I get her again.

John R.B. Eldridge, Huntsville. Jan. 4, 1822. The Nashville Whig, Emporium at Louisville, Ken. and Shawneetown paper, will give this four insertions and charge their accounts to the office of the Alabama Republican.

ILLINOIS GAZETTE, Shawneetown, Ill. Feb. 23, 1822

Ran away from the subscriber, about the 20th of December last, three negroes, to wit--one large mulatto fellow, named Richard, about 30 years of age, with very large whiskers, and thin hair on the crown of his head--had a side gun, and black slut, with some white in her face, also, lame in one shoulder. Also, his wife, Milly, a large bright mulatto woman, aged about 30 or 35, with straight hair and tucks on her head, her right foot has been burnt and toes injured. --They also took their daughter Phoebe with them--she is a very bright mulatto, about 9 years old, with blue eyes. I expect the above negroes are aiming for some of the free states, and perhaps have got a free pass, or may be conveyed off by some white person. Any person apprehending and delivering them to me in Limestone County, Alabama, or to any jail in the United States, so that I get them, shall receive the above reward, with all reasonable expenses. Information may be given to the subscriber by directing letters to Moorsville, Limestone County, Alabama. The Knoxville Register, Cincinnati Spy, Shawneetown paper, and Indiana Centinel, are requested to give the above three insertions and end their accounts as above. Jan. 23, 1822

ILLINOIS GAZETTE, Shawneetown, Ill. 30 March 1822

A ranaway negro, about 14 years old, calling himself Pete, came to Prince's Ferry, on or about the 5th January 1822--said he escaped from the steamboat Napoleon, and he belonged to a man named Cotton. The owner is requested to call and take him away.

P. Prince, Prince's Ferry. March 2, 1822

ILLINOIS GAZETTE, Shawneetown, Ill. 13 April 1822

$100 reward, in specie, ranaway from the subscriber, living in Fayette Co., Ky. on the 24th of May 1820, a negro man named Bill, now about 24 years of age, about 5 feet 7 or 8 inches high, rather slender made, but very nervous and active, of brown mulatto color, has two remarkable scars on his back just below one of his blade bones, one side not recollected, two or three inches long, occasioned by the strike of an ax--the other is rather a blotch on one of his cheek bones, about the size of a quarter dollar, darker than his other complexion. Bill is a plausible artful fellow, can read and write a tolerable hand, and no doubt, has a pass, and will attempt to pass as a free man, and by another name. His ears were pierced, and he wore leads in them when he went away. The above reward will be given if taken out of the state and brought home to me or $50 if secured in jail, and information given so that I get him.

Henry Rogers, Fayette County, Kentucky. March 22, 1822. The editors of the following papers are requested to publish the above four weeks and forward their bills to the editor of the Report for payment. Viz. Columbus Gazette, Vandalia Intelligencer, Shawneetown Gazette, and St. Louis Enquirer.

ILLINOIS GAZETTE, Shawneetown, Ill. May 4, 1822

Was committed on the 17th April last, to the jail in Golconda, a negro man, named Adam, about 60 years old, wrinkled and gray, says he came from Halifax Co., Va. He says he came on to the head waters of Holston and through Alabama, and belongs to the estate of one Scofield. The owner may prove him, or he will be hired out agreeably to law.

Amos Chipps, May 4, 1822

ILLINOIS GAZETTE, June 1, 1822

Ran away from the subscriber, living near Bardstown, Nelson County, the 2d of April, a negro man, named Abraham. He is about 23 years old, 6 foot high, stout, able bodied, weighing about 180 lbs. He is of a brown colour, he took with him two shirts, two pair of tow pantaloons, a lindsey roundabout; a lindsey waistcoat; a fur hat, about half worn, and also an ax. Any person taking the negro and delivering him in Morganfield jail or any other place that I can get him, shall be entitled to the above reward, and all reasonable expenses paid.

Thomas Mattingly, May 6, 1822

ILLINOIS GAZETTE, June 1, 1822

Was committed to my custody, on Saturday, the 11th instant, to be dealt with agreeably to law, a negro, Nathan, about 18 or 20 years old, 5 feet 5 or 6 inches high; had on, so he says, when he left his master, a blue roundabout and pantaloons of the same. He says that his master is by the name of Joseph Frazer, that he was moving to the state of Missouri, and that he left him some little distance from the ferry, in Kentucky opposite Shawneetown, Illinois. The owner is directed to prove and take him away or he will, after the expiration of six weeks, be hired out according to law.

Richard T. Jones, Sheriff, Shawneetown, Ill.
May 16, 1822

ILLINOIS GAZETTE, Shawneetown, Ill. July 6, 1822

Taken up, and committed to my custody, on the 18th day of June 1822, a negro man, who calls himself James, supposed to be a runaway, said boy is a dark mulatto, supposed to be 21,22 or 23 years of age, 5 feet 8 or 9 inches high; his hands are quite black, his face and breast more bright; a full round face; a scar of one inch in length over his right eye, in the edge of his hair; a small scar in his breast, which he says was done with a knife. Said boy says he broke the jail at Golconda some weeks past. Says he is free, but has lost his certificate; has a pass with the signature of Lasiby which pass he owns to be counterfeit. Says Alexander Joiner, who was put in jail at Golconda, gave the forged pass. Said boy has on a pair of blue striped twilled pantaloons, a striped cotton waistcoat, cotton shirt, no hat, is a sensible, arch fellow, his right jaw is much swelled, he says, produced by a cancer. If no owner applied for said boy in six weeks, he will be hired out as the law directs.

D.A. Richardson for D. Hay, Sheriff of White County, state of Illinois. June 12, 1822

ILLINOIS GAZETTE, Shawneetown, Ill. Aug. 3, 1822

$100 reward. Broke out of jail at Golconda, a negro man, who calls himself James Henry Jones (his real name is Armstead) about 5 feet 10 inches high, about 20 years old, dark yellow complexion, has a scar over his right eye, his two upper foreteeth out, clothing not known, has a bushy head of hair, has a pert mode of speaking. Any person securing said negro will receive $100 dollars reward, as I can secure him. Nathan Marders. Living within about 10 miles of Louisville, Jefferson Co., Ky.

ILLINOIS GAZETTE, Shawneetown, Ill. Aug. 10, 1822

Ran away from the subscriber, on the 4th of last Sept., a negro man by the name of Jim. He speaks broken language in the African tongue--he is stout built, 5 feet 8 inches high, dark complexion, he has a knot on one of his arms below the elbow. No other marks recollected. I will give $50 if secured in any jail, so that I get him again, or $75 if delivered to me four miles south of Huntsville. N.B. He formerly belonged to Samuel Parker of Charleston, S.C. and was brought here by Henry Gatewood.

James Cooper. Nashville Whig, Shawneetown Gazette, and Cincinnati Gazette will insert the above twice, and forward their accounts to the office of the Alabama Republican. Aug. 10, 1822
- -
ILLINOIS GAZETTE, Shawneetown, Ill. Sept. 21, 1822

Ran away from the subscriber, on the 15th of March last, a negro named Nat, aged 23 years, about 5 feet 8 or 9 inches high, is what commonly called a black negro, but is a little tinged with yellow--has a large flat nose, with a kind of bridge across it--stutters a little--has a bushy head of hair, and when travelling very much, his ankles are inclined to swell a little. He is a tolerable intelligent negro, and I expect will alter his name. The above reward will be given if delivered to my house, three miles from Port Royal, and 38 miles from Nashville, Tenn. or $50 if confined in any jail, so that I get him again.

Orren D. Battle. N.B. This boy calls himself Nathan. Sept. 21, 1822
- -
ILLINOIS GAZETTE, Shawneetown, Ill. Sept. 21, 1822

Forty dollars reward. Ran away from the subscriber, in June 1821, a likely negro fellow, named Phill, about 32 years old, about 6 feet high, a little yellow complected--has a very small scar on his forehead--also two other scars, made by the cut of an ax, one on one of his hands, and the other on one of his feet. It is very likely that he has procured a free pass, and may attempt to pass as a freeman. The above reward will be given if secured in any jail in the United States, so I get him again, and all reasonable expenses paid, if delivered to me in Clarksville, Tenn.

William R. Nelson, Aug. 31, 1822
- -
ILLINOIS GAZETTE, Shawneetown, Ill. Nov. 16, 1822

Ran away from the subscribers, living at the Tennessee Iron Works, Dixon County, West Tennessee, about the 22nd of Aug. last, a negro man by the name of Taff, 23 or 24 years of age, 5 feet 8 or 9 inches high, has a scar on his right cheek, occasioned by a burn; he has a rising on the back part of his neck, indicating king's evil. He is what may be called a black negro, his countenance pleasant, and a boy of uprightly turn and good sense. He has worked at the coaling business, and will probably offer his services to blacksmiths as a collier. The above runaway was taken up by the sheriff of Daviess County, Ky., on the 21st Sept. and deposited in the jail of the same county, at the Yellow Banks, from whence he made his escape, on Friday night, 4th Oct. inst. and it is supposed has gone either to Illinois, Indiana or Ohio. Any person who may take up said runaway, and secure him in jail, so that we get him again, shall be entitled to the above reward if taken in the state of Ohio or Indiana, if taken in Illinois, $75-- Kentucky, $50, Tennessee, $25--and all reasonable charges paid if brought home.

Anthony VanLeer & Co. Oct. 17, 1822--The editors of the Indiana Gazette, at Corydon, Evansville Gazette, Evansville, Inquisator, Cincinnati, Ohio and Illinois Gazette at Shawneetown, will insert the above in their respective papers for six weeks, and forward their accounts to Bernard VanLeer, Esq. Nashville for payment.

ILLINOIS GAZETTE, Shawneetown, Ill. Nov. 23, 1822

$100 reward, in specie, ran away from the subscriber, living in Fayette County, Ky. a negro man named Charles, about 27 years old, 5 feet 10 inches high, stout built, yellow complexion, lost his left thumb to the first joint, has a large scar on his right breast, occasioned by a cut of a knife, fresh done, very fond of whiskey. He has on a drab frock coat. I give the above reward if taken out of state, or $50 if taken within it, and all reasonable charges on the delivery or having him secured in any jail, so that I get him.

Jeremiah Rogers, Sept. 11, 1822--The editors of the following papers are requested to publish the above four times and send their bills to the editor of the Kentucky Gazette for payment: Franklin Intelligencer, Missouri Gazette, Columbus, Ohio, Intelligencer, Vandalia, Gazette, Shawneetown, Illinois, St. Louis Enquirer.

ILLINOIS GAZETTE, Shawneetown, Ill. 23 Nov. 1822

Ran away from the subscriber, living 3 miles east of the Big Spring, on the night of the 11th instant, a negro man named John, (he calls himself John Marshall), he is a very likely bright mulatto, about 23 years of age, 5 feet 5 or 6 inches high--he is a carpenter by trade, and no doubt will try to pass for a freeman, as he has made the attempt before--he has a remarkable scar on his breast, just below the buttoning of his shirt collar and has the appearance of having been occasioned by a burn, but says it was from the kick of a horse, his back is considerably scarred by a whipping he received the day previous to his going off--he had on when he went away a new homespun cotton shirt, an old pair of blue broadcloth pantaloons, very much patched, a dark cloth coat much worn, took with him a pair of white woolen homemade pantaloons, a wool hat much worn. The above reward of $50 will be given, if taken out of this state, so that I get him or $25 if taken in the state. All reasonable expenses paid if brought home.

John Hogan, Franklin Co., Ala. Oct. 12, 1822

ILLINOIS GAZETTE, Shawneetown, Ill. 30 Nov. 1822

Ran away from the subscriber, living in the vicinity of Limestone, Alabama, on the night of the 29th of May, two negro men, viz. Daniel, a bright mulatto, 22 years of age, about 5 feet 10 inches high, has a down look, speaks rather blunt, and would be apt, if questioned close, to betray himself by his countenance. He carried off with him a wool hat, half worn, and homespun clothes, he has very long hair, his upper lip very peaked, no scar marks recollected, in all probability he will try to pass for a free man, and change his name as he has done before. Frank, a black man, about 30 years of age, 5 feet 8 or 10 inches high, with one eye out, not certain which, but I believe his right, lame in his left foot by being frost bitten: his left big toe much larger than the right, his hair and beard a little gray, has but few teeth, and them very long, no other marks recollected. He was seen in company with the above negro, Daniel, near the Tennessee line. They were lately brought from Virginia, and it believed they are trying to make their way back to some free state. I will give the above reward to any person who will

secure them in jail or in like purportion for either,
and if delivered to me, all reasonable expenses paid.
Hardy Robinson, Sept. 12, 1822

ILLINOIS GAZETTE, Shawneetown, Ill. 16 Nov. 1822

Ran away from the subscriber, on the night of
the 8th June 1822, from my plantation on the forks of
Cypress, near Florence, Lauderdale County, Ala.,
Claiborn and his wife Charity. Claiborn is a very
likely negro man, about 5 feet 10 or 11 inches high,
remarkably well made, his features formed more like
those of a white man than a negro, has rather down
look and is slow spoken, he is an intelligent cunning
fellow; was owned by Mr. James G. Martin of Nashville, for about 10 years, and from whom he generally
hired his time until last winter, when I purchased
him. Charity is a small yellow wench, very well
formed, about 26 or 28 years of age, very light
complexion, long black hair and teeth; she was owned
by Mr. Thomas Martin, near Nashville, and was also in
the habit of hiring her time until I purchased her
last winter. They had so much clothing of different
kinds, I cannot describe what kind they may probably
be seen in. They took out of my lot two horses, which
returned the second day after they went away. I am
inclined to think they will push for those free
states, and probably descend the Tennessee River. The
above reward of $200 will be given for both, or $100
for either of them, if taken and secured so I get
them, and if delivered to me, all reasonable charges
paid.

James Jackson, Florence, Sept. 13, 1822--The
editors of the Louisville Public Advertiser, Cincinnati Inquisitor, Illinois Intelligencer, Edwardsville
Spectator, and the paper printed at Shawneetown, will
publish the above three times, and send their accounts to this office for payment. (Note: This is the
second group this particular owner lost within a
year's time. See pages 25 & 26.)

ILLINOIS GAZETTE, Shawneetown, Ill. 18 Jan. 1823

Ran away from the subscriber, in Logan County,
Kentucky, about the 1st of October last, a negro man
named Joe; about 22 years old, 5 feet 8 or 10 inches
high, very stout build, very short thick neck, and
small head, large shoulders, very dark complexion,and

when walking, appears to be lame, has a scar on the inside of one of his ankle bones, caused by the cut of an axe, down look and very impudent. He has worked at the tanning and blacksmith business. The above reward will be given for his apprehension if taken out of this state or $25 if taken in this state, and all reasonable expenses.

William T. Duncan. The editors of the Illinois Gazette, Shawneetown, and Edwardsville Spectator will please insert the above advertisement three times in their respective papers and forward their accounts to this office for collection. Nov. 2, 1822

ILLINOIS GAZETTE, Shawneetown, Ill. 18 Jan. 1823

Was committed to the custody of the sheriff of Edwards County, on the 13th day of November 1822, a black woman, named Sally, who, if not claimed according to law, will be hired out as the law directs. Said Sally is about 33 years of age, 5 feet 4 inches high, and has a large scar under her chin.

For H.J. Mills, Sheriff, per John B. Johnson, D.S. Anthon. 15 Nov. 1822

ILLINOIS GAZETTE, Shawneetown, Ill. 1 March 1823

Ran away from the subscriber, living in Greene County, Illinois, a negro man, named Nat, (but has changed his name, since his elopement to Georgia) He is about 5 feet 8 or 10 inches high, thick and well made, large thick lips, little yellowish complexion, had on, when he went away, a pair of leather pantaloons, and a red linsey shirt, had with him an old rifle gun. I suspect he will make for the Ohio saline or Caldwell County, Kentucky. Any person that will apprehend said negro, and give information to General White, at the Saline, or the subscriber, in Greene County, shall be rewarded for all expenses and trouble.

Thomas Rattan. Feb. 15, 1823--The Illinois Gazette will publish the above 2 times and forward his account to the Illinois Intelligencer office for collection.

ILLINOIS GAZETTE, Shawneetown, Ill. 13 March 1823

Ran away from the subscriber, on Friday the 14th of March, a negro man named John. He is about 20 years of age, 5 feet 7 or 8 inches high, a mulatto, heavy built and somewhat bowlegged, carried with him a full suit of blue broadcloth and other clothing. He went in company with a negro man, who has two sets of free passes, and calls himself William Jones, who can read and write, and will probably forge or alter a pass or certificate of freedom for John. Any person delivering the said John to me or confining him in any jail so that I can get him, shall receive the above reward, if he is taken out of state, or $25 if taken within the state.

Robert D. M'Lean, Shawneetown, Ill. 13 March 1823

ILLINOIS GAZETTE, Shawneetown, Ill. 26 April 1823

Ran away from Simeon True, where he was hired, in Scott County, on the 22d of this month, a negro man named James, belonging to the heirs of J. Cooper, deceased, he is about 30 years of age, quite black, thick lips, shows his teeth very much when spoken to, his upper foreteeth are quite open, about 5 feet 10 inches high, his weight about 180 lbs. He had on, when he went away, a green cloth coat, black pantaloons, and a wool hat, but will, no doubt, change them--his other clothing not known. It is supposed he was persuaded away by a worthless white man, about 26 years of age, who left the neighborhood about the same time. Two or three other negroes are believed to be in company with them. The above reward and all reasonable charges if taken out of the state and returned to the subscriber, or secured in any gaol or $30 if taken in the state and secured as above, so that I get him. He will no doubt change his name.

Daniel Cooper, guardian for the heirs of J. Cooper, dec. March 22, 1823--To be inserted in the Cincinnati Advertiser, Cleveland Herald, and Shawneetown Gazette, and the editors bills to be forwarded immediately to the office of the Kentucky Reporter.

ILLINOIS GAZETTE, Shawneetown, Ill. 17 May 1823

Ran away from the Naper's Iron Works, Dickson's County, Tennessee, where they were hired on the 1st inst. and are now running at large in Logan County, Kentucky, two negro men of the following description: one about 35 years of age, named Toby, of common height, of the darkest complexion, and homely features, walks lame, has clothing, one brown linsey frock coat, two close body coats, mixed linsey black and white, one or two pair of pantaloons of the same, all double wove, one pair black casimere pantaloons, two or three shirts, and pantaloons mixed in the chain with flax and cotton, and filled with all cotton. The other is likely bright mulatto, about 21 years of age, named Lewis, of common height, but rather spare built, blue eyes, and commonly stutters in speaking--he has a long coat nearly down to the heels, of dark plain linsey, two blue linsey coats, double wove, two pair linsey pantaloons, one double and the other single wove; other clothing not recollected, except one pair pantaloons and one shirt just out of the loom, mixed in the chain with flax and cotton, and filled with all cotton. They may change their clothing, or their names where they are not known. It is presumed they may continue in Logan County for some time, and frequently and privately visit Russelville, where they are both well acquainted, or may attempt to cross the Ohio River. I will give $50 for the two, or $25 for either, if taken in the bounds of Logan County; if taken out of the bounds of Logan and the adjoining counties, and within the district of one hundred miles of Russelville, I will give $100 for the two, or $50 for either if taken beyond the distance of one hundred miles from Russelville. I will give the above reward for the two or $100 dollars for either and pay all reasonable charges if delivered to me in Logan County or lodged in any jail of the different distances, and notice given me so that I get them again. The money shall be paid in current bank notes of the state of Kentucky, except they return to the works and give themselves up where they might be.

Henry Ashburn, Logan County, Ky. April 10, 1823
The editors of the Whig, Nashville, Tenn., Illinois Gazette, Shawneetown, and Spectator, Edwardsville, Ill. are requested to insert the above advertisement three weeks and forward their accounts to the office of the Weekly Messenger, Russelville, Ky. for collection.

ILLINOIS GAZETTE, Shawneetown, Ill. 28 June 1823
Notice. Was committed to jail on the 2d day of June inst., a negro man, who at first called himself Reuben, but now says his real name is Bob. Said negro

is a stout well built fellow, about 25 years old, 5 feet 10 or 11 inches high, has a stoppage in his speech, and is quite impertient, has a scar above his left eye, is well clothed in blue linsey, and says he belongs to the estate of William Mars, deceased, late of Logan County, Kentucky. Unless he is demanded and proven, by the proper owner, in six weeks, he will be sold out according to law in such case made and provided.

Henry Dubois, Sheriff, Lawrenceville, Lawrence Co., Ill. June 9, 1823

ILLINOIS GAZETTE, Shawneetown, Ill. 5 July 1823

$50 and all reasonable expenses paid to stop the runaway that I get him again. Sawney, a black fellow, 5 feet 10 or 11 inches high, 30 years old, weighs about 175 pounds, a tolerably likely boney fellow, one foretooth out, a scar or burn on his right temple, when walking, he stoops forward and appears to limp a little, speaks plain and distinct; rather of a haughty cast of mind when questioned with boldness--he can read and write a little. He and his white wife are both fond of spirits. He is a tolerable good shoemaker, sawyer and a good hand at any kind of farming work. He is a fellow whom I raised near the town of Nashville, Tenn.; he never travelled much, never 50 miles from home. It is thought they are aiming for some of the free states, Ohio, etc. and it is believed they have gone down the Cumberland River. He took several pieces of clothing with him, to wit: a coat of blue jeans, three shirts, one a coarse linen ruffle shirt, three or four pair of pantaloons, one pair of shoes, two pair of coarse socks, one half worn wool hat, one or two black striped waistcoats, it is believed that they keep their clothing in a long basket. The clothing of his wife not recollected except a calico sun bonnet, she is a very white negro, so much so, that not many people would suspect her to have any negro blood in her. She is about 30 years old, and weighs about 120 pounds, her eyes are rather of a blueish gray, with a film or speck in one of them, and both appear to be sore--one or two of her teeth are affected, and, with all, she is a great drunkard--her name is Betsy. She has two children, but is unknown whether she carried them with her or not; both were white mulattoes, the

40

youngest is supposed to be 7 or 8, and the other 10 or 12 years old--both are girls. Betsy has passed as a free woman here. They ran away on Saturday night the 14th last.

John Boyd, Nashville, June 20, 1823--The editors of the Independent Press, Cincinnati, the Fredonian, Chilicothe, and the Shawneetown paper will please insert the above advertisement twice, in their respective papers, and forward the account to the office of the Nashville Gazette for settlement.

ILLINOIS GAZETTE, Shawneetown, Ill. 26 July 1823

Ran away from the subscriber, living in Robertson County, Tennessee, on Tuesday night, the third last, a negro man, named Jupiter. Supposed to be about 45 years of age, rather under the middle stature, quick sparkling eyes, quick spoken and possesses a rather smiling countenance when spoken to. Also at the same time a negro wench, named Frank, supposed to be about 24 years of age, very black, about the middle size, well made and very likely. I will give the above reward for the two, if taken in the state or $25 if taken out of the state and delivered to me living on the road leading from Clarksville to Nashville, and all reasonable expenses paid.

Marven Lowe, July 7, 1823--The printers at Hopkinsville, Ky. and Shawneetown, Ill. will publish the above three times and forward their accounts to the office of the Watchman, Clarksville, Tenn. for payment.

ILLINOIS GAZETTE, Shawneetown, Ill. 6 Nov. 1823

Ran away from the subscriber, living one and a half miles from Nashville, on the night of the 28th inst. two negro men, named Jim and Elijah; Elijah is about 40 years of age, 5 feet 8 or 10 inches high, of dark yellowish complexion, a very flat nose, and his face much wrinkled, has two large scars from cuts on his head, which is not perceivable unless his hat is off, he has a variety of clothing all of which is not recollected; but had a new fur hat, a blue broadcloth coat, a pair of mixed grey pantaloons, a new roundabout summer coat, domestick and fine shirts, it is uncertain what clothing he may be found in possession of as he had a great many clothes. It is likely he may have a free pass. It is believed he will endeavor to get through Kentucky, by way of Matisonville, to Illinois or Indiana. Jim is about 32 years old, 5 feet 6 or 7 inches high, a large beard, speaks very quick when questioned. Had on when he eloped a domestick shirt and pantaloons, a wool hat, his shoes much worn, his other clothes not recollected. I will give a reward of $20 for each of the above negroes, if taken within the state of Tennessee, and $50 for each or either of them if taken out of Tennessee, and all reasonable charges. If brought to my hosue, or secure in any jail so that I get them, payable in bank notes at the state of Tennessee.

Robert Baxter, Sept. 30, 1823

ILLINOIS GAZETTE, Shawneetown, Ill., 8 Nov. 1823

Taken up, by the subscriber, on the 29th of this instant, a black woman, who says her name is Jane; has no remarkable features; is about 30 years of age, says she is free, has no certificate of freedom. The owner, if any, is requested to prove property, pay charges and take her away--as she will be hired out at the expiration of six weeks, as the law directs in such cases.

D.H. Moore, Sheriff of Alexander Co., Ill. Sept. 29, 1823

ILLINOIS GAZETTE, Shawneetown, Ill. 20 Dec. 1823

Taken up and committed to the custody of the sheriff of Edwards County, on the 12th day of December instant, two black men who say their names are Frank and Mack. Frank is about 28 years old and about 5 feet 10 inches high. Mack is about 25 years of age and about 5 feet 6 inches high. Both dark complexion, have no remarkable features. The owner, if any, is requested to prove property, pay charges and take them away, as they will be hired out at the expiration of six weeks, as the law directs in such cases.

J.B. Johnston, D.S. Edwards County, Ill. 13 Dec. 1823

ILLINOIS GAZETTE, Shawneetown, Ill. 24 Jan, 1824

Ran away from the subscriber, living on the waters of the Obion River in Henry County, Tenn., a negro man, named Bob, about 30 years old, very black, about 5 feet 10 or 11 inches high, well made, with a scar on his nose and upper lip. He is a tolerable

good barber, an excellent hostler, and is very polite
fellow. He had, when he went away, a tolerable pair
of whiskers. Any person delivering or securing him in
any safe place where I may get him again, shall
receive the above reward.
John H. Dorlan, 3 Jan. 1824

ILLINOIS GAZETTE, Shawneetown, Ill. 3 April 1824
Taken up, committed to my custody on the 12th
inst. a black man who says his name is Dick, he is
about 5 feet 7 inches high, slender made, had on when
taken, a blue roundabout jacket and linsey pantaloon-
s--says his master's name is Kerby, that he left said
Kerby near the mouth of Ohio, 2nd Sept. last. The
owner is requested to prove property, pay charges and
take him away as he will be disposed of as the law
directs in such cases.
D.H. Moore, Sheriff, Alexander Co., Ill.

ILLINOIS GAZETTE, Shawneetown, Ill. 10 April 1824
Taken up, committed to the jail of Franklin
County, state of Illinois, on the 28th of January,
one negro man who says his name is John, he is about
20 or 21 years of age, about 6 feet high, dark complexion, has no remarkable features, rather knocked
kneed, he says he belongs to Charles Poke, the owner
if any, is requested to prove property, pay charges,
and take him away, or he will be hired out at the
expiration of six weeks as the law required in such
cases.
D.W. Maxwell, Sheriff, Frankfort, Ill. 25 Jan.

ILLINOIS GAZETTE, Shawneetown, Ill. 24 April 1824
Carried off, by some white men, two negro men,
on the 21st of March by the name of Clemmens and Lem.
Clemmens is a stout, well made boy, about 20 years of
age, black with a large mouth and thick lips--about 5
feet 6 or 8 inches high. He had on, when he went
away, a surtout coat of broadcloth, white pantaloons
and shirt, several other articles of clothing not
recollected. Lem is about the same age and height of
a light complexion, well made, small eyes with one
tooth out before--his clothing consists of homespun.
They crossed Tennessee, four miles above Branim's
Ferry at which place he called one of the negroes by
the name of Tom and the other Jim. They stole a canoe

43

and made down the river, as is supposed. The man that
had them is of a spare make, dark hair, sandy whiskers, with part of his left ear off. I will give $20
for the white man, and $50 for the negroes or $25 for
either of them--delivered to me on the north fork of
the Obion, Henry County, or securing them in any jail
so that get them again.

John H. Dorlan, April 5, 1824

ILLINOIS GAZETTE, Shawneetown, Ill. 10 July 1824

Taken up and committed to my custody on the 23d
day of June 1824, two negroes of the following description. One woman named Olly about 28 years old,
dark complexion; also one girl, about 12 years of
age, yellow complexion. The owner, if any, is requested to come and prove them, or otherwise at the
expiration of six weeks, they will be dealt with
according to law.

D.W. Maxwell, Sheriff, Franklin Co.

ILLINOIS GAZETTE, Shawneetown, Ill. 21 Aug. 1824

Ran away or stolen from the subscriber, in
Montgomery County, Tenn., a negro man, named Jo,
about 25 years of age, about 5 feet 10 inches high--a
high forehead. He left my farm the 12th of January
last in Dickson County; he was pursued and overtaken
about 22 miles below the mouth of the Cumberland, in
the state of Illinois, in the employment of Nathan
Norman, who left Dickson County about the time the
negro absconded, and it is believed he persuaded the
said negro to go off. The negro was brought to the
mouth of the Cumberland, then broke custody from the
agents of the subscriber, handcuffed since that time
he has not been heard of. The above reward will be
given for the delivery of said negro in Montgomery
County, or $25 for his confinement in any jail, where
the subscriber can get him--all reasonable expenses
will be paid. The negro man belongs to the estate of
Benjamin Cox, deceased.

Winiford Cox, Admx. June 12, 1824

ILLINOIS GAZETTE, Shawneetown, Ill. 18 Sept. 1824

Was committed to my custody, on the 16th inst.
two negroes, one a man by the name of Arthur, about 5
feet 8 or 9 inches high, about 30 years of age, of a
black complexion, rather bow legged, no unnatural or

44

accidental marks observable. The other a woman named Henny, of a black complexion, about 38 or 40 years of age, about 5 feet 7 inches high, rather fleshy and robust, no perceivable scar or accidental mark. The above named negroes having failed to establish their right as free black citizens upon being takenup as runaway negroes, will be dealt with as such according to law.

Andrew Kuykendall, Deputy Sheriff of White County, Ill. 19 July 1824

ILLINOIS GAZETTE, Shawneetown, Ill. 18 Sept. 1824

There has been committed to my custody, a negro man, by the name of George, 35 or 40 years of age, near 6 feet high, has no remarkable scars or marks, has no beard except on his upper lip. Said negro will be hired out, agreeably to the law concerning runaways, unless the owner shall substantiate his claim within two months from this date.

Daniel Hay, Sheriff of White County, Ill., Carmi, 14 Aug. 1824

ILLINOIS GAZETTE, Shawneetown, Ill. 18 Sept. 1824

This day there was committed to jail a negro man, who calls himself Douglas Duckson; aged about 29 years, about 4 feet high, rather yellow complexion, high forehead, a little marked with the small pox on the face. Says he belongs to James Davis at Chickasaw Bluffs.

A. Chipps, Sheriff, 27 July 1824

ILLINOIS GAZETTE, Shawneetown, Ill. 2 Oct. 1824

Pope County vs. People of the State of Illinois. To the sheriff of Pope County, Greeting: Whereas Abel G. Larison and Amasa Davis, this day brought before me a negro man, named Ezekiel, and on examination, he appeared to be a runaway; therefore you are hereby commanded to take him, and him safely keep until discharged by law. Given under my hand and seal, this 11th day of Aug. 1824.

Francis Jones, J.P. seal. I do certify the above to be a true copy, this 13th day of August 1824. Henry Slanford.

ILLINOIS GAZETTE, Shawneetown, Ill. 9 Oct. 1824

Was taken up, on the 28th inst. and now in my

custody, a mulatto man, who calls himself Jess, and says he belongs to Ranson R.H. Burnes, living in Wilson County, Tenn. He is about 25 years of age, 5 feet 11 inches high, spare made, rather inclined to be round shouldered, has no particular marks or scars. When he was taken, he had the following articles of clothing: blue cloth frock coat, half worn, a jeans vest, blue mixed, a homespun cotton shirt, one pair black casimere pantaloons, and vest of the same; one pair cotton pantaloons, one cotton shirt, one jeans coat, blue mixed, one pair wool socks, one pair shoes, heels plated with iron, all of which were about half worn. Also had with him a silver watch, one shot gun, one razor box and strap, one silk handerchief, and money purse, 37 cents in cut specie, and two large hawk bill knives. The owner is requested to come forth, prove property, pay jail fees and take him away. If he pleases, or he will be hired out as the law directs.

James Hall, Sheriff of Hamilton Co., Ill. McLeansboro, 30th Sept. 1824

ILLINOIS GAZETTE, Shawneetown, Ill. 20 Nov. 1824

Was taken up, by James A. Richardson, at the Saline, and committed to jail by Metacha Willis, a justice of the peace to and for the county of Gallatin, a dark mulatto man, who calls himself, Charles Butler, and says he comes from Huntingdon County, Penn., and is a free man, but has no papers with him to establish his freedom. He is about 5 feet 8 inches high, has with him a very considerable amount of clothing, among which is a scarlet vest, grey coat and pantaloons, and sundry articles of summer clothing; also $19 and 50 cents in specie. The owner, if the negro is a slave, is requested to come forward, prove his property, pay charges and take him away. Otherwise he will be dealt with agreeably to the statute provision of this state.

Henry Boyes, Sheriff of Gallatin Co., Ill. Shawneetown, Nov. 20, 1824

THE SANGAMO JOURNAL, Springfield, Ill. 12 July 1832

Ran away from the subscriber on Thursday the 26th of April last, two negro men, Ben and Reuben-- Ben is about 40 years of age, short and heavy made, of a yellow complexion, 5 feet 9 or 10 inches high, plays on the violin; with both his ears off close to his head, which he lost for robbing a boat on the Ohio River. No doubt but he has changed his clothing since he left home. Reuben is heavy well built fellow, about the same height, and what may be called a black negro, about 30 years of age, has a down look when spoken to, one of his fingers next to the little finger is off to the first joint, which hand not recollected, and walks lame occasioned by a pain in the hip.

I will give $50 for either of them, or $25 each if caught in 30 miles of my residence, or secured in any jail so that I can get them, or all reasonable charges if brought home and delivered to me, living in the state of Kentucky, and county of Livingston, near the head of Hurricane Island, Ohio River.

James Ford, July 12, 1832

THE SANGAMO JOURNAL, Springfield, Ill. 9 Feb. 1833

Ran away from the subscriber, on Wednesday, the 13th inst., a negro man, named Stephen, about 27 years of age, 5 feet 10 or 11 inches tall, knockneed, and walks with his toes much turned out, shows his teeth when he laughs, speaks English and French, stammers when questioned, and is rather simple, is a little hard of hearing, has had a sore on his left eye. Had on when he went away a short blue cloth soldier's coat, tow linen shirt and pantaloons and hat, as he has other clothes with him. I will give the above reward for apprehending the said negro, securing him in the jail at Belleville; $15, if taken out of St. Clair County and secured in any jail; and $20, if taken out of the state and secured in any jail so that I get him again.

John Hays. St. Clair County. Dec. 19, 1832

THE SANGAMO JOURNAL, Springfield, Ill. 9 Nov. 1833

Stop the runaways--$100 reward, if taken without the state of Missouri, and $50 if taken within the state for the following described negroes who went off together on Saturday night, the 26th of Oct., to wit: Tom, a very black fellow, 23 years of age stout and likely--well supplied with clothing; had a black cloth coat and leather pantaloons, an impudent spoken fellow, and no doubt the leader of the band. Lewis, of a bright yellow complexion, had a blue cloth coat and pantaloons, an old janes coat, 23 years of age, common negro height, likely and heavy built, a piece of his under lip lately bitten off, may not be well yet. Hiram, a black fellow, about 20 years old, stout and likely, had an old plaid cloak with sleeves, a blue coat cut off short, a pair of leather pantaloons and a pair of red stripped pantaloons; has a small scar on his forehead, and has a remarkable whining tone of voice. The above reward will be paid for the aforesaid negroes, or a proportionable paid for one or two of them delivered to the subscriber, or safely lodged in jail, so that we can get them again. A letter addressed to either of us at Canton, Lewis County, Missouri, will be attended to promptly.

Abner Bourne, Geo. Railey, Isaac Westerfield.
Oct. 31, 1833

WESTERN INTELLIGENCER, Kaskaskia, Ill. 22 May 1816

Ran away from Glasgow, Barren Co., Ky, in August last a negro man named David, who it is supposed, will attempt to get into some of the northwestern territories, he is 22 or 23 years of age, 5 feet 10 inches high, well made, has a scar on his nose, small eyes, and complexion rather darker than common, he can read and write and has in all probability written himself a pass as issued from the Clerk of Surry Co., Virginia, purporting his freedom; he will I expect pass himself as a painter having lived with one for several months previous to his elopement and done some of the coarser work. The above reward will be given for delivering said fellow to me in this place, or $50 and all reasonable charges that I can get him again.

B.B. Winn

WESTERN INTELLIGENCER, Kaskaskia, Ill. 29 May 1816

Ran away from the subscriber on the morning of the 2d inst. a negro man who calls himself Brookens Cole. He is about 35 years of age, 5 feet 9 inches and a half high, very strongly formed, short, flat nose, and has two of his foreteeth of the left upper jaw out, and a scar on his left eye brow and has a larger scar on his right arm, near the shoulder, talks very broad; he took with him the following clothing, viz. a leather roundabout and pantaloons, a domestick manufactured blue coat, striped domestic overalls, rorum hat, new linen shirt, and a pair of new shoes; some evil disposed person may have furnished him with a pass to enable to travel unmolested as a freeman. Whoever will take up said negro and lodge him in any jail and give information so that the owner can get him, or will deliver him to me at Mine Shibboleth, Washington County, shall be entitled to the above reward, with all reasonable charges. I do hereby forewarn all persons from harboring said negro, being determined to punish those who are found guilty.

Joseph M'Clenahan, Mine Shibboleth, April 6, 1816

WESTERN INTELLIGENCER, Kaskaskia, Ill. 19 June 1816

Ran away from the subscriber on the 13th inst. a negro fellow named Randal, 5 feet 6 or 7 inches high, about 28 years of age, good features, smiles when spoken to or in speaking, stutters in talking, knock kneed, turns his toes out very much when he walks; crippled in his right hand, took with him a couple of linen shirts, a pair of overalls of the same and a shirt and overalls of deer skin and an old wool hat.

The above negro crossed into the Illinois territory at Smelser's Ferry, on the night of the 1st inst. Any person securing said negro in any jail so that I get him in possession again, shall receive the above reward, or the reward and all reasonable charges if delivered to me in St. Charles.

Robert Spencer, St. Charles Co., Mo. Territory, 5 June 1816

WESTERN INTELLIGENCER, Kaskaskia, Ill. 24 July 1816

I have taken up a negro man, supposed to have runaway from his master. He calls himself Tom, is about 20 years of age, 5 feet 5 1/2 inches high, black and well made, with large hands and feet. Has with him a pair of velvet or corded pantaloons, a pair of buckskin pantaloons, a pair of blue jersey pantaloons, faced with deerskin, a black casimere roundabout, a striped cotton vest, buckskin hunting shirt, and white hat. He came to this place in a boat and passed himself as a freeman. This notice is given that the owner, if he be a slave, may obtain his property.

Josiah Millard, St. Genevieve, July 22, 1816

WESTERN INTELLIGENCER, Kaskaskia, Ill. 24 July 1816

Ran away from the subscriber at Cumberland Furnace, Dickson Co., Tenn., some time in May 1813, a negro man named Carey, but has since changed his name to Buck, and will change his often as he changes his situation. He is a likely stout well made young fellow, about 26 or 27 years old, of a copper color; his height not known but supposed to be 5 feet 9 or 10 inches high, large made to his height; his feet broader across the toes than common; intelligent, but not remarkable for honesty or industry. He descended Cumberland River in a keelboat to the mouth, there shipped himself on board Capt. Blackman's barge as a hand to Cincinnati, but at Louisville unshipped himself and travelled by land in company with a man that lived at that time 15 miles from Brownsville, Penn. as far as Chilicothe; there detained some time. It is probable he has since passed to Pittsburg, or some part of the state of Pennsylvania, or the state of Ohio, or perhaps the adjacent territories. He had a forged pass in the name of some gentleman in the neighborhood of Chilicothe with permission to hire himself and said he was returning home. I will give the above reward for him if lodged in jail, and information given to me so that I get him, and reasonable expenses paid if brought home.

Montgomery Bell, July 2, 1816 (This is the same fellow who lost some other slaves in 1820.)

WESTERN INTELLIGENCER, Kaskaskia, Ill. 24 July 1816

Ran away from me at the same place, on the 20th June 1816 a young negro fellow, named Bob, about 22 or 23 years old, of middle size and of a copper color. As well as I recollect his middle toes on both his feet contracted by corns; had on when he ran away a home manufactured mixed cloth coat, with wire metal basket buttons, but will no doubt change it the first opportunity; the balance of his clothing, not recollected. If caught, neither will acknowledge to whom they belong, but will try to make their escape if not securely ironed and taken care of. I purchased Bob of Maj. David Smith, on the Elk Fork of Red River--he formerly belonged to Mr. Fredric Hise of Russelville,

Ky. may return to that place; but is presumed he will attempt to get to Pittsburg, then up the river Ohio in a boat as a hand, or by land, as he says he has relations in Pittsburg. I will give the above reward to secure him in jail and give me information so that I get him, and reasonable charges if brought home.

Montgomery Bell, 2 July 1816

WESTERN INTELLIGENCER, Kaskaskia, Ill. 14 Aug. 1816

Ten dollars reward will be given for the apprehension and delivering to me in Hopkinsville, Ky., my negro man, Squire, or confining him in any jail so that I get him again, and all reasonable expenses paid. He is 22 years old--a bright mulatto, has very much the appearance of an Indian; his hair is nearly straight, about 5 feet 10 inches high, stammers a little when spoken to angerly, and has very sly down look--had on when he went away a pair of white cotton pantaloons and blue mixed cotton coat; his other clothes not recollected. He may attempt to go down the river as he has done before runaway and went to New Orleans; he is a brick layer by trade and may attempt to get there again. All persons are forewarned from harboring said negro and all masters and owners of boats from taking him out of the country. The above reward will be given if confined in any jail so that I get him again, or $20, if delivered to me in Hopkinsville, and all expenses paid.

James Terry, 20 July 1816. The editor of the St. Louis Gazette is requested to give the above advertisement three insertions and forward his account to J. Terry for payment. Editors.

WESTERN INTELLIGENCER, Kaskaskia, Ill. 6 Nov. 1816

Ran away from the subscriber about the 20th of Sept. a negro man named Esau from the United States Saline, when he went away he had on tow shirt and pantaloons, and blanket cape. He is of a moderate dark complexion, and about 5 feet 11 inches high, very trim and round built, a high forehead, and an expressive countenance when spoken to, and has a very smooth way of expressing himself; he has been a preacher for several years in the Methodist society. The above reward will be given to any person that will deliver him to me or confine him in any jail either in state or territory, and if confined in jail, I can receive information at Shawneetown, Illinois territory.

William M'Mahon, 21 Oct. 1816. The editors of the Reporter, Lex., Ky., Argus, Frankfort, Ky. and the St. Louis Gazette are requested to insert the above advertisement two months in their respective papers, and send their accounts to this office for collection. Editors.

WESTERN INTELLIGENCER, Kaskaskia, Ill. 14 May 1817

Stolen from the undersigned sometime in the month of November last, between the Wabash River and the Saline Creek, a mulatto girl, 12 years old. I sent her with an Indian girl to hunt some horses, the latter of which was found dead apparently killed by the limb of a tree; but the other has never been heard of since. It is supposed that she has been stolen by some person and carried off. Said mulatto girl took with her a speckled roan stallion, bald faced, white mane, red tail and glass eyed, branded on the left thigh. A money reward of $50 will be given to any person who will deliver said girl to me, in this place, with a reasonable allowance, for the expenses what may be incurred, or a handsome reward for giving information where she is.

Louis Decoungne, Kaskaskia. April 21, 1817

WESTERN INTELLIGENCER, Kaskaskia, Ill. 9 Oct. 1817

Taken up by the under subscribers, two negroes, one a negro man named Ben, the other a negro woman, named Betsy, man and wife, both belong to Col. Henry Walker, living in Rockingham Co., Va., as they say and committed to jail in Kaskaskia, Randolph Co., Illinois territory; about 33 years of age. The owner is requested to come and prove property, pay charges and take them away.

George Fisher, Pierre Bono. Sept. 26, 1817

WESTERN INTELLIGENCER, Kaskaskia, Ill. 15 April 1818

Stop the runaway. $50 reward. Ran away from the subscriber on the 23d of March last, living in the county of St. Genevieve, in Broisbrula bottom, a negro man named Green, 5 feet 7 or 8 inches high, yellow complexion, supposed to be about 25 years old and of a pleasant countenance. He had on when he went away a bear skin big coat, and a new fur hat, and other clothing not necessary to mention and $50 or $60 in money. It is supposed he is in the Illinois territory and may likely want to pass himself as a freeman. Any person delivering to me the above negro man or lodging him in jail so that I get him, shall receive the above reward.

Joel Kinnison, April 9, 1818

WESTERN INTELLIGENCER, Kaskaskia, Ill. 13 May 1818

Ran away from the subscriber on St. John Point, Lahadle Twp., St. Louis County, Missouri Territory, on the night of the 27th April, a mulatto boy, named Mace or Mason, about 18 or 19 years old, low of stature, tolerably heavy, took with him 2 or 3 suits of clothing, a new hat and buffalo robe. He started in a canoe down the Missouri. The above reward will be given to any person securing said negro in any jail, and information given thereof to the editor of the Missouri Gazette or the subscriber, so that I get him again.

Harly Sappington.

WESTERN INTELLIGENCER, Kaskaskia, Ill. 2 Sept. 1818

Ran away from the subscriber in the state of Mississippi about 14 months ago, a negro man named Obediah, about 30 years of age, 6 feet 1 or 2 inches high, the right eye smaller than the other, and appears to be deficient, dark complexion. Said negro was lately in jail at St. Louis, but broke out and has made his escape, and is supposed to be now in this territory. The above reward will be given for apprehending and putting him in any jail so that I can get him again; whoever should apprehend the said negro will be so good as to inform me per mail, directed at Natchez post office.

Alexander ? Rae, Aug. 28, 1818

WESTERN INTELLIGENCER, Kaskaskia, Ill. 23 Dec. 1818

Ran away from the subscriber, in Morgan County, state of Georgia, a negro man named Dick, about 45 years old, black complexion, his beard somewhat gray, about 5 feet 8 or 9 inches high, stoutly built, somewhat knockneed, his toes turning rather outward; he has lost some of his jaw teeth, which may be seen when laughing, has rather a down look, his eyes somewhat red, speaks plain, and artful in telling a

story. Being about to be detected in his villany, no
doubt but that he thought it best to make his escape;
he is a proficient hand in stealing and concealing,
and robbing of houses, as he regards neither doors or
locks; he left the subscriber on the 15th of August
last--took with him a knapsack made of homespun cotton bagging, buttoned up with red, one roundabout
blue broadcloth coat, blue cloth pantaloons--grey
corded pantaloons, blue raise stripe casimere waistcoat, yellow tollinet waistcoat, two hats, one fur,
the other wool, with other clothing not recollected;
he is a very good shoemaker, and will probably work
at that business, or at the whipsaw, as he intends
passing himself for a freeman. A negro answering his
description was seen passing the Cherokee nation
about the 28th August, who had a paper purporting to
be a free pass; no doubt that he intends travelling
to the state of Ohio, if not already there. Any
person apprehending and delivering him to me, or
confining him in any jail so that I can recover him,
shall receive $100--If the villain is apprehended
within the states of Ohio, Illinois or Indiana, and
secured in any safe jail so that I can get him again,
the above reward will be given.

David Love, 21 Nov. 1818

WESTERN INTELLIGENCER, Kaskaskia, Ill. 14 April 1819

$100 reward for apprehending a negro man by the
name of Ezekiel, about 6 feet high or upwards, very
black, 22 years old, formerly belonging to Field
Bradshaw, near Edwardsville. He has some pretensions
of freedom which have been encouraged by a certain
Petty Ligoner by the name of Pugh who resides in
Edwardsville. Pugh encouraged him to leave Edwardsville and run to Kaskaskia, where he promised to follow
and protect him, which he did until I purchased him.
I put him in the possession of three men to take to
his home, from whom he escaped, and I presume he will
try to get to Edwardsville to his protector. I am
determined to prosecute any person who will harbor
said negro, with full vigor of the law. And I will
give the above reward to any person who will deliver
him to me or my agent at Fort Massac.

Isaac D. Wilcox, 14 April 1819--The editors of
the Illinois Emigrant will insert the above advertisement 3 times, and forward their account.

WESTERN INTELLIGENCER, Kaskaskia, Ill. 9 June 1819

Ran away from the subscriber, on the night of the 13th ultimo, a negro man named Charles, about 24 or 25 years of age, of large stature--he has a small piece of his ear taken off. He stole from my desk $180--a hundred dollar bill on the bank of Nashville, other bills not recollected. Also a negro woman named Peggy, this fellow's wife, run away at the same time, near the same age--She is a common sized woman, very black and has lost the sight of one of her eyes.

James Adkins, June 9, 1819--The editors of the Emigrant, Shawneetown, and Enquirer, St. Louis are requested to insert the above advertisement three times, and forward their accounts to this office for collection.

WESTERN INTELLIGENCER, Kaskaskia, Ill. 9 June 1819

Ran away from the subscriber, on Saturday evening the 29th of May, a negro man named Harry, aged about 28 years, about 5 feet 11 inches high, very stout built, uncommonly large under lip. Had on when he went away a brown great coat (the lower part torn off) with a large cape, check shirt, new roram hat, and new linen trousers, and took with him one check shirt and one pair striped trousers. A liberal reward will be given for apprehending said runaway, and delivering him to the subscriber at Milton, in Madison County, on Wood River, for confining him in the nearest jail, so that he may be recovered--He was purchased about 3 months since at Harrisonville on the Mississippi. He is supposed to have passed through Kaskaskia on Tuesday evening the 1st June, on the road to Vincennes.

Robert Collet, June 9, 1819

WESTERN INTELLIGENCER, Kaskaskia, Ill. 14 July 1819

Ran away on the 10th of June from the subscriber, living in St. Genevieve, a negro man named Baptiste, about 36 years of age, 5 feet 8 inches high, dark complexion, well made, and speaks the French and English languages--had on when he absconded, a grey cloth coat, and buckskin overalls.--He has a mother living in Prairie du Rocher, and two brothers in Kaskaskia. The above reward will be given to any person that will secure the said negro in jail or otherwise.

J.B. Bossier, 7 July 1819

WESTERN INTELLIGENCER, Kaskaskia, Ill. 28 July 1819

Ran away from the subscriber the 12th inst. living on the Missouri, near Marthasville, two negro men, the one black, 28 years old, 5 feet 8 or 9 inches high, a down look, bad countenance, with a blemish in one of his eyes, had on tow linen shirt and pantaloons, and a drab full cloth coat--the other a yellow or mulatto, 18 or 19 years old, 5 feet 7 or 8 inches high, had with him a tow linen shirt and pantaloons, blue broadcloth coat and pantaloons, and checked gingham pantaloons; they may likely change their clothes and make for the state of Illinois, and pass for freemen. They had a rifle with them.

Any person apprehending them and bringing them to me at Martinsville shall have the above reward or securing them in any jail so that I get them, shall have $50 or $25 dollars for each.

Benjamin Young, Marthasville, Mo. Terr. 17 July

WESTERN INTELLIGENCER, Kaskaskia, Ill. 4 Aug. 1819

Ran away from the subscriber the 27th instant, a negro man named James Gardner, about 5 feet between 3 or 4 inches high, his color somewhat of the yellowish cast--his person slender, his weight about 135; he is considerably bowlegged; has a scar in the center of his forehead immediately under the hair; his upper foreteeth much decayed; possesses a remarkable store of religious knowledge; inclined in his tenants to the methodist persuasion, has their book of discipline, a hymn book, a catechism and an almanac, in all which, he is ostentious of displaying his knowledge--his age about 30. He had on, when he eloped, a half worn wool hat, a very pale blue cotton coat, a tow linen shirt, pantaloons of the same kind and a pair of new bound shoes.

Whoever will apprehend and commit the said James Gardner to prison, in the town of St. Genevieve, or deliver him to the subscriber living on the Saline Creek, about 8 miles down its confluence with Mississippi, shall receive a reward of $40, if taken within the county, $50 if apprehended elsewhere.

Obediah Scott, St. Genevieve, Mo. Terr. 28 July 1819

56

WESTERN INTELLIGENCER, Kaskaskia, Ill. 4 Aug. 1819

In June last (the 25th) a negro man named Dick run away from my plantation in the Missouri territory, near the town of Louisiana, Pike county. He is about 5 feet 8 or 9 inches high, tolerablely stout made, about 21 or 22 years of age, very black and remarkably ugly; has a small scar on his forehead (perhaps he has a scar on his breast perceivable) occasioned with the cut of a knife; he has a very singular shaped foot, very narrow at the heel and broad across the toes; his eyes generally red--he is fond of spirit and will steal.

He was taken up at Herculaneoum about the first of July last, and committed to jail for attempting to commit a rape on a white woman. He broke jail about the 2 of July, and was taken on the road leading from Herculaneoum to St. Genevieve, but broke away. It is supposed he will attempt to get into the states of Illinois or Indiana, or perhaps to New Orleans, as there was a canoe stolen about 6 miles below St. Genevieve, supposed to be taken by him. Any person who will secure him in any safe jail, or give information to me or Aaron Garnsey near Herculaneoum so that either of us may get him, shall receive the above reward.

David Garnsey, Pike County, Mo. Terr. 28 July 1819. (See page 16 for other notice.)

WESTERN INTELLIGENCER, Kaskaskia, Ill. 29 Dec. 1819

Ran away from the plantation of the subscriber in Sumner Co., Tenn., about the 25th of August last, two slaves, a negro fellow and mulatto boy. The fellow named John, about 30 years old,...had had his back well scarred with whipping...The boy named Ellick, about 13 or 14 years old, well grown and stout made, his color that of a bright mulatto though his hair indicates him to be more than half negro, has grey or hazel colored eyes...

David Shelby. (Poor copy on this notice.)

WESTERN INTELLIGENCER, Kaskaskia, Ill. 22 July 1820

A runaway negro taken, who says his name is John, about 34 years of age, about 5 feet 5 inches, his color of the deepest shade of African negro, his visage narrow. He says he formerly belonged to David Shelby of Tennessee. The above fellow was apprehended

near this place on the night of the 10th last, and is
committed to the jail in Randolph County and will
there remain until claimed pursuant to the "act rega-
rding free negroes, mulattoes, servants and slaves.",
and a reward of $10 in apprehending and all other
fees are paid.

J.W. Gillis, Coroner, Randolph Co., Kaskaskia,
20 July 1820

WESTERN INTELLIGENCER, Kaskaskia, Ill. 7 Aug. 1820
Ran away from the subscriber in Wilkes Co.,
Georgia, in Dec. 1818, a negro by the name of Jess
(age unclear) 5 feet 8 or 10 inches high, his complexion a little yellow, and has a small win or lump on
his forehead. He is a good wagoner and plays the
fiddle. I am apprehensive he was conducted off by a
man calling himself Kilk. I will give $100 reward for
information so that I get him again.

William Kilgore, Feb. 1820. All printers in
Alabama, Mississippi, Illinois and Louisiana are
requested to insert the above once a month for three
months: the Nashville Gazette, Franklin Monitor
(Tenn) and the Reporter, Lexington, Ky. once, and
forward their accounts to the post master at Washington, Wilkes Co., Georgia for payment.

WESTERN INTELLIGENCER, Kaskaskia, Ill. 9 Sept. 1820
Public notice. I have in the common jail in
Randolph County, at this time a negro man, named Joe,
committed upon a warrant of Miles Hotchkiss, one of
the justices of the peace in and for said county, as
a runaway. He is about 22 or 23 years of age, 5 feet
6 or 8 inches high, very black, has some scars on his
forehead, which he says he got by fighting--good
countenance, his nose rather short, and sharper than
common to negroes. This fellow was brought from the
state of Kentucky af few weeks ago by Doctor William
L. Reynolds and traded to a man by the name of Pensa-
no in St. Louis, who he says is his owner at this
time.

Samuel E. Christy, Sheriff of Randolph Co.,
Kaskaskia, 1 Sept. 1820

WESTERN INTELLIGENCER, Kaskaskia, Ill. 23 Sept. 1820
Ran away from the subscriber, living on Platten
Creek, in Missouri, about 5 miles from Horines Mill,

58

on the 9th July last, a negro boy named Bill, about 19 or 20 years old, 5 feet 9 or 10 inches high, very black, has a very remarkable scar on his under lip, occasioned by a bite. He formerly belonged to Titus Strickland of New Bourbon, St. Genevieve County. Shortly after he ran away, he broke into a house and stole a broadcloth coat, a pair of white dimity pantaloons, shirt and vest, and a pocket book, with $12 in silver and some notes of hand in it. The above reward will be given if secured in jail so that I get him again.

James M'Cormack, Jefferson County, Missouri, Sept. 20, 1820

WESTERN INTELLIGENCER, Kaskaskia, Ill. 7 Oct. 1820

Ran away from the subscriber, at the town of Illinois, opposite St. Louis, about the 1st of August last, a mulatto woman, known by the name of Harriet Hewlett, between 40 and 45 years of age, marked by the small pox, and has the appearance of an Indian. The above reward will be paid to any person who will deliver her to me at this place or $10 if lodged within any jail in this state and all reasonable charges paid.

Ephraim Town, Illinois, Sept. 21, 1820

WESTERN INTELLIGENCER, Kaskaskia, Ill. 16 Jan. 1821

Public notice is hereby given that I have in confinement at this place a negro man, who calls himself Jim, committed as a runaway on the warrant of Miles Hotchkiss, Esq., one of the justices of the peace in and for Randolph County, state of Illinois. Jim is about 6 feet 5 or 6 inches high, between 25 and 26 years old, middling stout made; he says he was brought from the state of Tennessee within the limits of this state about 6 years ago by a Mr. Isom Harris, who resided near M'Farland's Ferry on the Ohio and was taken to the state of Missouri some time in the month of Oct. last by said Harris, who, he says, lives within 3 or 4 miles of St. Michael at this time.

The owner or master of said negro is requested to come forward within six weeks from the date hereof and substantiate his slave, or he will be disposed of, according to the statute of this state made and provided in such cases.

S.C. Christy, Sheriff of Randolph County, Kaskaskia, 4 Jan. 1821

ILLINOIS INTELLIGENCER, Vandalia, Ill. 30 Sept. 1831
Ran away from the subscriber on Sunday evening the 18th Sept. a mulatto man, named Claiborn, about 25 years of age, 6 feet high, stout made, a very bright mulatto, his teeth rather broad, has a down cast look when spoken to, has worked at the confectionary business, and may pass for a pastry cook; had on when he went away, a light round jacket, a buff vest, dark casimere pantaloons, and a half worn fur hat; he took with him sundry articles of clothing, among which a black broadcloth coat, half worn, pitched under the arm, ground shirt, one with a plated linen bosom; he can read a little, and is supposed to have forged free papers and making his way to Canada. The above reward will be given for his apprehension and delivery in St. Louis or $30 if secured in any jail so that I can get him. Information to be left with Valrin & Reel or Luther Morgan, St. Louis, Sept. 28, 1831

ILLINOIS INTELLIGENCER, Vandalia, Ill. 30 Sept. 1831
Was committed to my custody as a runaway on the 5th day of Aug. 1831, a negro man, about 34 or 35 yeares of age, a bright mulatto, and says his name is Willis, and that he belongs to Edward Swanegin, in Monroe County, Georgia--Also on the 21st day of August, a yellow boy, about 21 years of age, blue eyes, tall and slim, and calls his name Ishail, and says he belongs to Amenuel Hanny, McMinn Co., East Tennessee. The owners are requested to come forward, prove them, and take them away, else they will be hired out agreeable to law.
A.J. Storm, Sheriff of Pope County, Aug. 25, 1831

ILLINOIS INTELLIGENCER, Vandalia, Ill. 25 Aug. 1831
Ran away from the subscriber, some time in October last, then living, in Covington, a negro man, a slave for life, called Sam. I have reason to believe that he has been, since his absence from me, lurking about the premises of Old Lyd in St. Clair and Hartshora White in Washington County. He is too well known in these parts to need any further descri-

ption. I will give a liberal reward for his commitment to any jail so that I can get him, or for any
information respecting him, leading to his apprehension.
N.M. McMurdy, Vandalia, Aug. 27, 1831

THE WESTERN VOICE, Shawneetown, Ill. 23 Dec. 1837
$50 reward. Runaway from the subscribers, near
Gallatin, Sumner County, Tenn., on the 19th July, a
bright mulatto man by the name of Vetal, 5 feet 5 or
6 inches high, stout made, a little stooped in the
shoulders, and a little knock need, large thick
hands; took with him a coarse cotton shirt and pantaloons of gingham, shirts one a red striped, the other
brown white, casimere pantaloons, dark roundabout
jacket, and black fur hat; took his clothing in a
travelling carpet bag. He will no doubt try to pass
himself for a free man, and steward of a steam boat.
He is by profession a cooper and rough carpenter. The
above reward will be given if he is confined in any
jail so we get him.
Eli Odom, Jesse Cage, Dec. 23, 1837

VOICE AND JOURNAL, Shawneetown, Jan. 5, 1839
Was committed to my custody as sheriff of Pope
County, Illinois, a negro man by the name of Jef,
about 25 years old, very black, heavy made, and
weighs about 150 lbs. The owner is requested to come
forward, prove his property, pay charges and take him
away, otherwise he will be dealt with according to
law.
Isham Clay, sheriff, Nov. 17, 1838

VOICE AND JOURNAL, Shawneetown, Jan. 5, 1839
There was committed to the jail of Union County, Ill. on the 15th of October 1838, a mulatto man
who calls his name Anderson Cherry. He is about 21 or
22 years of age, about 5 feet 5 inches high, he has a
scar across his nose, he has a suit of blue jeans
cloths, wears a white hat; no other marks discovera-
ble, and states that he belongs to Daniel Cherry of
Haywood County, West Tennessee. The owner is requested to come and take said negro out of jail within
six weeks or he will be dealt with according to law.
Wiley J. Davison, sheriff, Nov. 17, 1838

VOICE AND JOURNAL, Shawneetown, Ill. Jan. 5, 1839
Ranaway from the subscriber in Lafayette County, Mississippi, a negro man named Tom, aged about 20, a black or dark copper color, about 5 feet 11 inches high, stout and well made; the big toe on the right foot rather larger than the other, a slight stoppage in his speech when spoken to; took with him, round crown wool hat and a black fur hat half worn; other clothing not recollected. The above reward will be given for the securing said boy in jail so that I get him, and reasonable expenses for delivering him to me near Oxford, Mississippi.
Joshua T. Brown, Nov. 19, 1838

RANDOLPH COUNTY RECORD, Sparta, Ill. 18 March 1846
Was committed to my custody on the 29th day of January 1846, a negro boy, calling himself Frank, about 21 or 22 years old, 5 feet 5 1/2 inches in height, weighs about 140 pounds, considerably scarred with the whip, appears reserved; had on when committed two pairs pantaloons, one light mixed jeans, the other blue jeans; old blue jean coat, old black furred hat, and coarse shoes; dark complexion; says he is from Evansville, Indiana. The owner, if any, of said negro, will come forward, prove property, pay charges and take him away, otherwise he will be dealt with as the law directs.
A. Dearduff, sheriff Union County, Ill. Jonesboro, Feb. 2, 1846

THE SPARTA REGISTER, Sparta, Ill. 1 Aug. 1849
Broke custody, near Murphysboro on the 14th inst., a negro man, supposed to be about 26 years old, 5 feet 5 inches high; heavy set and of a copper collor; a scar on his right hand, as if caused by a burn. He had on when he left, a blanket coat, and a black silk hat, and left in my possession a horse, saddle, bridle and buffalo robe, and calls himself Jack Jones. I will give $10 to any person who will apprehend and deliver him to me at Murphysboro.
John Elmore, sheriff, Jackson Co., Ill. 18 July 1849

SPECTATOR, Edwardsville, Ill. 17 July 1819
Ran away from the subscriber, a negro man named George, and took with him his wife and three of his

children, viz. Isbel, a girl about 12 or 13 years of age; Charles, a boy about 6 or 7 years of age; and the least, a girl about 3 years of age, rather inclined to be yellow. The above reward will be paid to any person who apprehend said negroes, and return them to the subscriber.

Colden Williams, Howard County, M.T. June 21

SPECTATOR, Edwardsville, Ill. 4 Sept. 1819

Ran away from me on the 21st Aug. 1819, in Pike county, near the town Louisiana, a likely negro boy, named Joshua, about 21 years old, and about 5 feet 8 inches high; had on a pair of corderoy pantaloons, domestic coat, etc. a tolerable good hat--complexion rather on the yellow. He was taken up at St. Charles on the 25th and put in jail on the 27th. He broke jail and made his escape. The above reward will be given by me to any person who will deliver the said negro boy to the sheriff of St. Charles County.

Hugh Gorden, Sept. 4

SPECTATOR, Edwardsville, Ill. 2 Nov. 1819

Notice is hereby given that I have at this time, in the common jail of St. Clair county, two negro men, committed by virtue of a warrant issued by Henry J. Good, one of the justices of the peace in and for said county, taken up and brought before him as runaways; and in obedience to the said warrant, and agreeable to the laws of this state in such cases made and provided, I committed them accordingly, to be dealt with as the law directs. One of them named John, about 24 years of age; five feet high, he has on his nose a scar, he is well made; talks with good sense. The other is named William. He is about 27 years of age, about 5 feet 9 inches high. He has on his left hand a number of warts; he also has on his upper lip a scar visable. He talks with reason, appears active, and well read. They have some little clothing with them, of no great value. They say they belong to George Smith, in Nashville, Tenn.

William A. Beaird, sheriff of St. Clair County, state of Illinois, Belleville, Oct. 6, 1819

SPECTATOR, Edwardsville, Ill. 25 April 1820

Ran away from Chariton, Howard County, M.T. on the 18th March, a negro man named Jim, lately

63

belonging to Capt. Ramsey of New Madrid. Said negro is about 5 feet 8 or 9 inches high, middling well featured, weighs about 165 pounds, and is middling black. He took with him a dog and gun. Said negro was sold to subscriber on the day of his elopment. He was raised by Joseph Beatty, of Howard County. The above reward will be paid to any person who will secure said negro in any jail if taken without the territory; or $35 if taken within the territory, so that I can get him.

Charles Simmons, Chariton, M.T. 18 March 1820

SPECTATOR, Edwardsville, Ill. 2 May 1820

Ran away from the subscriber on the night of the 26th instant, a negro man named Peter, commonly calls himself Peter Johnson, of black complexion, about 30 years old, about 5 feet 9 or 10 inches high, stout made and clumsy in his motions; pretends to be religious, and can read a little. Has on one of his arms a deep scar, occasioned by a burn; when closely interrogated, stammers very much. His clothing was a dark brown cloth coat and pantaloons with gilt buttons; scarlet cassimere vest; shoes nearly new, the soals of which are fastened on with pegs. Also a negro woman named Ellen, about 27 years old, black complexion, of good size and well formed, answers very pleasantly when spoken to. Had a considerable quantity of clothing, particularly of fine articles. Also a negro woman named Sylvia, of black complexion, about 25 years old, of good size, stout made and pleasant countenance; took with her many articles of clothing, particulary fine articles. Also a negro boy, black complexion, about 10 years old, named Martin, lisps much when speaking; had on a plain linsey roundabout and flesh colored cassimere pantaloons. They will probably direct their course for the state of Illinois.

The above reward will be given for the four if taken out of the territory, and confined in jail so that we can get them again, or $50 for each. If taken in the territory and confined as aforesaid, $100 for the four, or $25 for each.

Justus Post,
Sam'l B. Sydna.
Bonhomme, St. Louis County, M.T. March 29

SPECTATOR, Edwardsville, Ill. 13 June 1820

I have in the common jail of St. Clair County, at this time, a negro man, named Isaac, committed upon the warrant of Edmund P. Wilkinson, one of the justices of the peace in and for St. Clair County, as a runaway. He says he is about 21 years of age, about 5 feet high, slender made, very black, his features regular; he talks much, and his right ankle has been hurt. He says he belongs to James Adkins, near Kaskaskia, this sixth day of June 1820, Belleville.

William A. Beaird, sheriff of St. Clair County, June 13

SPECTATOR, Edwardsville, Ill. 17 October 1820

For sale, an indentured negro man. The above negro is about 23 years of age, and has 13 years to serve; is well acquainted with farming; a pretty good rough shoe maker, and has attended at a distillery; and possesses a good moral character. For further information, apply to the printer. Oct. 17

SPECTATOR, Edwardsville, Ill. 28 August 1821

Ran away from the subscriber, about 3 weeks since, a negro fellow named Bill. He is not very black, is 5 feet 10 inches high, stout made, thin face, very talkative, but when spoken to has a down look; when walking he turns his toes very much out, and makes a track broadest across the middle. He broke Montgomery jail on the 24th inst. The above reward will be given for securing him in any jail so that I get him, if apprehended out of the state, or $30 in the state.

Fredrick A. Bradford, Chariton, Missouri, Aug. 28

SPECTATOR, Edwardsville, Ill. 26 February 1822

I have confined in the common jail of St. Clair County, at this time, a negro man taken up as a runaway, and committed on the warrant of James Mitchell, Esq. by the name of Jackson Anderson, from Culpepper County, in Virginia. He appears to be about 55 or 60 years of age; heavy made, and has a piece bit out of the upper part of his right ear, and has a scar under his left eye, done by the kick of a horse. He says he is a freeman.

This 13th day of Feb. 1822. William A. Beaird,

sheriff of St. Clair County, Feb. 26

SPECTATOR, Edwardsville, Ill. 14 May 1822

Ran away from the subscribers, living in Pike County, Missouri, on the 16th inst. a negro man named Berry, very black, 5 feet 9 or 10 inches high, speaks quick, and stammers when confused; had on when he went away a shirt of negro cotton clothes, but had several changes.

The above reward will be given to any person who will secure said negro in any jail, so that the subscribers get him again.

John S. Wilson, Samuel Wilson. April 20.

SPECTATOR, Edwardsville, Ill. 18 May 1822

Ran away from the subscriber, about the last of January, a negro girl named Sib, about 5 feet high, bright mulatto, pleasing countenance, tolerably fleshy, and about 28 years of age. She had a variety of clothing with her, composed principally of the best she had, having, left all her coarse clothes behind her. This girl was in a family boat bound down the river, but in consequence of the ice the boat stopped on the Illinois side of the river opposite St. Louis; after remaining there for some time, the girl made her escape, owing to the facility with which she could run away, being in a free state. I will give $30 reward for her apprehension and safe confinement in any jail within 30 miles of St. Louis, or for her delivery to me in said town.

Hayes Rawls, St. Louis. Feb. 23

SPECTATOR, Edwardsville, Ill. 19 November 1825

Ran away from me in Franklin County, Alabama, on the 26th of August 1824, a negro man, Thornton, by name, sometimes calls himself Keys, no doubt will assume other names; age about 28 or 30; quite black; rather lean; about 5 feet 10 inches high; boasts of his manhood; has many small scars on his face like scratches, and some on his head; the underpart of one of his ears gone, and rather notched; a hard countenance; coarse, strong voice; pretty large breast, adn tapers down; he says he lived a part of two years as a free man, near Shawneetown, Illinois, and followed the distilling business. This time should have been in or about 1822 or 23. Any person who will deliver him to me at home, will receive $100 reward or $50 to give information so I get him. He no doubt descended the Tennessee River from Florence.

J. Cockrill. Oct. 11th, 1825

SPECTATOR, Edwardsville, Ill. 28 July 1826

Ran away from the subscriber on the night of the 22d instant, a negro man named Thomas, of the following description, to wit: black complexion, handsome features, about 6 feet high, square built, 25 or 26 years of age, took with him two suits of clothes, one black cloth coat about half worn--blue jeans, woollen pantaloons--one cotton coat, blue and yellow--one pair white cotton pantaloons--one white vest, and two shirts, and a black fur hat--one pair of shoes, and an old shot gun. The above reward will be given to any person who will apprehend said negro, and secure him in any jail so that I get him. Information to be given to me at Newport, Franklin County, Missouri.

John Gall. July 1825

THE ADVOCATE, Belleville, IL 23 June 1842

Committed to the jail of Monroe County, Ill. on the 4th day of June a.d. 1842, as a runaway slave, a negro or man of color, calling himself Chandler, bright mulatto, about 33 years of age, 6 feet high, slender made and without other pecularities or mark of description. The owner if any there be is notified, that unless said slave shall be claimed, he will be dealt with according to law in such case made and provided. Dated this 8th day of June 1842.

Also committed on the 27 of May 1842, as appears a dark mulatto man, about 35 years of age, 5 feet 8 or 10 inches high, heavy set, strong made, quick spoken, somewhat agitated when addressed and without other pecularities or marks of description, calls himself Aaron Douglas. His owner is requested to come forward and prove his property and pay charges within six weeks, or said negro will be dealt with according to law in such cases made and provided.

John Morrison, Sheriff Monroe Co. Waterloo. 7 June 1842

THE ADVOCATE, Belleville, Ill. 27 July 1843
    Committed on the 19th day of April last, a negro man who calls himself Henry, and says he belongs to John Thompson, living in the state of Louisiana. Said negro is about 5 feet 8 inches high, about 22 years old, dark complexion and weighs about 170 pounds; had on some old cotton clothes nearly worn out, and has a lump above his right eye. If the owner comes forward and proves property, pay charges he can have him or he will be dealt with according to law in such cases.
    John Steele, sheriff of Perry County, 29 June 1843

THE ADVOCATE, Belleville, Ill. 14 March 1844
    Was committed to the jail of St. Clair County, Illinois, on Tuesday the 5th day of March 1844, a negro man, who calls himself John Johnson, about 5 feet 6 or 8 inches high, and of very black complexion, and blind in the left eye, wears a gray box cassinet coat, dark cassinet pants, calf skin slippers and a fur cap. He is supposed to be about 25 or 26 years old, and says he lives in Cincinnati, Ohio. The owner is requested to come, prove property, pay all charges and take him away within six weeks, or he will be dealt with as the law directs.
    B. Million, jailor, Belleville, 7 March 1844

THE ADVOCATE, Belleville, Ill. 4 July 1850
    Committed to the jail of St. Clair County, Illinois, on the 27th of June 1850, a negro who calls himself James Clarey, 28 years old, 5 feet 5 or 6 inches high, a scar on his nose, caused, he says, by the kick of a horse. Clothing--white cotton shirt, yellow jeans pantaloons, brown summer cloth pea jacket, black cloth cap, and kidskin shoes, rather a pleasant countenance. His owner is notified to prove property, pay charges and take him away within six weeks from date, or he will be hired out for charges, as the law directs.
    Benjamin Million, jailor of St. Clair County, 4 July 1850.

THE ILLINOIS GAZETTE, Shawneetown, 15 Jan. 1825
    Ran away from the subscriber, living near Trenton, Ky. on the night of the first of this month, a

negro fellow named Henry; dark complected, 23 years old, 5 feet 5 inches high, well built, little inclined to be fleshy, speaks slow, mild and with a smile; lisps a little; has a fine set of teeth; handsome and polite, but easily confused, has on the back of his neck, just between the hair, two scars made by cupping; by trade a blacksmith. Took with him a dark purple frock coat, fulled, and reaching to his heels--two roundabouts, one dark, the other white, both jeans and filled with yarn; a pair of pantaloons, dark, filled alternately with cotton and yarn, which makes them appear striped, and has a gore in each, by extending from the ankle entirely up on the inside--blue broad cloth coat, and a half worn fur hat, a pair of boots and new stitch down shoes, double soled, and the upper leather in one piece. This fellow, probably, will aim for Indiana or Illinois. Any person who will apprehend said negro, and deliver him to me, or secure him in any jail, so that I get him again, shall receive the above reward in commonwealth paper.

Robert Christian, Nov. 13, 1824

THE ILLINOIS GAZETTE, Shawneetown, Ill. 29 Jan. 1825

Was committed to my custody, on the 27th just, by Ivy Reynolds, an acting justice of the peace in and for said county, a negro man, calling his name William Coles; 25 years old, 5 feet 4 or 5 inches high; a black complexion; a very soft, mild spoken fellow. He states that he understands the blacksmith's trade; had on a blue broad cloth coat, about half worn, also a waistcoat of the same, about half worn; a pair of blue mixed pantaloons, a white pair of cotton pantaloons, a shirt of the same quality, very coarse cloth, a pair of half boots about half worn. Also a surcoat, with snuff-colored lining. Given under my hand, this 29th Nov. 1824.

James Copland, sheriff Johnson County.

THE ILLINOIS GAZETTE, Shawneetown, Ill. 26 March 1825

Thirty dollars in Kentucky money will be given for apprehending and confining Isham, a negro fellow, who ran away from LaHay's salt works on Wednesday evening, the 23d inst. Isham is a bright black, about 5 feet 6 or 8 inches high and heavily made; between 20 and 26 years of age; had on, when he went off, a

drab colored roundabout, and I think hosey pantaloons. He will, I have no doubt, change his clothes.
He has no marks that I distinctly recollect of, but,
I think, he has a scar on his neck. He is a slow
spoken fellow, rather sulky and otherwise when interrogated, and cannot look up. I will give the above
reward if taken in the county, and pay all reasonable
charges, or $40 Kentucky money, and pay charges to
any person who will deliver said fellow in Shawneetown, or return him so that I get him.
        W.B. Dozier, March 26

THE ILLINOIS GAZETTE, Shawneetown, Ill. 26 March 1825
        There was committed in the jail of Pope County,
in the state of Illinois, this runaway on Wednesday,
the 9th March inst., a negro man, named Wilson; about
22 years of age; about 6 feet high; large person,
blackish color; the great toe on the left foot off at
first joint; has a large scar on the top of his nose,
extending the whole length thereof. The said Wilson
had on, when committed, a white linsey roundabout;
pantaloons made of hair and cotton cloth; twilled
striped cotton vest, and a new wool hat.
        Isham Clay, sheriff Pope County. N.B. The said
Wilson said he belongs to Geo. Dismukes, living on
Mascow's Creek, Davidson County, state of Tennessee,
and that he left his said master about 5 weeks ago.
March 15, 1825

THE ILLINOIS GAZETTE, Shawneetown, Ill. 2 April 1825
        Run away from the subscriber, living in David-
son County, Tennessee, on the 28th of January last, a
large negro fellow named Wilson. The said negro has a
scar on his nose, which is perceivable only when
closely examined; his left big toe cut off; has
uncommonly large and ugly feet; short neck, and his
feet turned out considerably--he remained in Todd
County four or five weeks, and I am apprehensive that
he has gone over to Illinois or Indiana--if any
person will secure the said negro for me in any jail,
in either this, or any other state, and advise me of
the same, by letter addressed to me at Nashville, the
above reward will be paid and all expenses.
        George R. Dismukes, 17 March 1825

THE ILLINOIS GAZETTE, Shawneetown, Ill. 14 May 1825
Ran away from the subscriber, about the 5th inst., a negro man named Charles; about 30 years of age; about 5 feet 5 or 6 inches high; stout made; yellow complexion. He has crossed the Ohio River, just below Shawneetown, and probably is about the Saline Lick. Any person that will take up the above mentioned slave, secure him in jail and give information to me, living near Morganfield, Union County, Ky., shall receive a liberal reward and if delivered, all reasonable charges paid.
John W. Waring, 23 April 1825

THE ILLINOIS GAZETTE, Shawneetown, Ill. 18 June 1825
There has been committed to my custody, a negro man, who calls his name, Tom. Says he belongs to David Dunn, formerly of Davidson County, Tennessee, and has now removed to the western district. Tom is about 30 years of age, 5 feet 9 or 10 inches high, no remarkable marks or scars. He will be dealt with according to law, at the end of two months, if no owner appears to claim him.
G.B. Hargrave, sheriff White County, Carmi, 21 May 1825

THE ILLINOIS GAZETTE, Shawneetown, Ill. 2 July 1825
There was committed to the jail of Pope County, on the 7th day of June 1825, a negro man, by the name of Ezekiel; about 5 feet 11 inches high; dark complexion. He says that he belongs to Isaac D. Wilcox, in the state of Illinois, Johnson County. No particular marks recollected.
Isham Clay, sheriff, 2 July 1825

THE ILLINOIS GAZETTE, Shawneetown, Ill. 2 July 1825
There was committed to the jail of Pope County, on the 25th of June 1825, a negro man, by the name of Joe; dark complexion, 5 feet 8 or 9 inches high; about 27 years old. He says that he belongs to James Bailey, living in Mississippi state, Pipkin's County, that he left his master about last Christmas.
Isham Clay, sheriff, 2 July 1825

THE ILLINOIS GAZETTE, Shawneetown, Ill. 27 Aug. 1825
Golconda, 23 July 1825. Broke jail, on the 20th of this instant, at night, a negro man by the name of

Joe. He was committed on the 25th of June last.
    Isham Clay.

THE ILLINOIS GAZETTE, Shawneetown, Ill. 27 Aug. 1825
    Ran away from the subscriber, living now at
Columbus, in Mississippi, a negro man, named Joe, and
taken up some time in June last, in Pope County,
Illinois, and broke jail, and made his escape from
there on the 20th of July. He has a scar, from a
stab, just above one of his hip bones. He is about 27
or 30 years old, 5 feet 6 or 8 inches high; black;
has rather a down look when spoken to; his eyes have
rather a red cast; spare built but neatly formed--and
no particular marks other than as above described.
Before leaving the jail, he told another negro that
he would not tell his right name, nor acknowledge the
name of his master again, as it was from his having
done so, in this instance, that he came to be taken
up, and news of it went to me. I have reason to
believe that he is aiming for the state of Ohio. I
will give the above reward to any person who will
apprehend said negro, and put him in jail, so that I
can get him, or $100 to have him delivered to me,
where I now live, and will pay all expenses for
transportation.
    James Bailey, Shawneetown, 22 Aug. 1825

THE ILLINOIS GAZETTE, Shawneetown, Ill. 27 Aug. 1825
    Taken up and committed to the custody of the
subscriber, a negro boy, says his name is Charles
Cochran; about 19 or 20 years of age; has a remarkable scar upon his breast, occasioned by a burn; one on
his left arm; also one on the right side of his face,
which has the appearance of being done recently by a
bruise or hurt. He says his master's name is James
Walker, residing near Perryville, Perry County, Tennessee. He will be hired out, according to law, at
the expiration of six weeks, if no owner appears.
    Henry   Boyers,   sheriff   Gallatin   County,
Shawneetown, 27 Aug. 1825

THE ILLINOIS GAZETTE, Shawneetown, Ill. 27 Aug. 1825
    Ran away from the subscribers, living on the
Yellow Creek, Dickson County, Tennessee, on the 5th
instant, 4 negroes, viz: Dave, Adam, Sharper, and
Ridley. Dave is 65 or 70 years of age; about 5 feet 7

72

or 8 inches high; quick spoken, and very polite. No other marks recollected. Adam, 40 years of age, about the same height; several of his foreteeth out; a scar on his forehead. a nick in one of his ears; bowlegged; a little round shouldered. He had a stone bruise on the ball of his foot, rather callous and required to be paired, or he cannot walk without limping. Sharper, 35 years of age, 6 feet high; very black, and sour countenance. No other marks recollected. Ridley, 22 years of age, about 5 feet 7 or 8 inches high; walks with his toes turned very much out. Any person apprehending the above negroes, and securing them so that we can get them again, and giving information to either of the subscribers, at Palmyra, Montgomery County, Tennessee, shall receive the above reward, or $20 for each.

John Wilson, Dorothy Goodrich.

THE ILLINOIS GAZETTE, Shawneetown, Ill. 27 Aug. 1825

There has been committed to my custody, a negro man, who calls his name, William Griffy; says he belongs to James Baker, who lives about 4 miles from Millersburgh, Bourbon County, Ky. William is supposed to be about 20 years of age; 5 feet 6 or 8 inches high; when spoken to, has rather a down look. No remarkable marks or scars. He will be dealt with according to law, at the end of two months, if no owner appears to claim him.

H. Boyes, sheriff Gallatin County. Shawneetown, Aug. 23, 1825

THE ILLINOIS GAZETTE, Shawneetown, Ill. 10 Sept. 1825

Was committed to the jail of Johnson County, on the 20th inst. two negro fellows, as runaway slaves, of the following description to wit: one of them is a bright mulatto, about 25 years old; 5 feet 7 or 10 inches high; fierce sneer spoken, but easy detected if interrogated; has small scar on his right cheek, and severely marked on his back with the whip. The other is of a dark complexion, 17 or 18 years old; his teeth is remarkably wide apart; of singular speech, and if closely examined, a scar or mark may be perceived under this right eye. They say they belong to John Lowery, of Tennessee, in Jackson's Purchase--they call themselves Nickison and Scott.

J. Copland, sheriff. Aug. 22, 1825

THE ILLINOIS GAZETTE, Shawneetown, Ill. 17 Sept. 1825
Committed to my custody, in Wabash County, on the 26th July last, a negro man, who calls himself Alfred; of dark complexion; 5 feet 6 inches high; about 22 years of age. He stated he was raised in North Carolina; that his master there joined the Quakers and freed his blacks, etc. If no owner appears, he will be dealt with according to law.
A. Armstrong, sheriff Wabash County. 6 Sept. 1825

THE ILLINOIS GAZETTE, Shawneetown, Ill. 17 Sept. 1825
Was committed to my custody on the 30th inst., a runaway negro man, who calls his name, William Nelson; says that he is free since the death of his master, whose name, he says was John Cowden; that he died at Natchez some time in June last. Said negro is about 5 feet 11 inches high; has two small scars on his cheek, and one on his nose; had on a check shirt, linsey roundabout and pantaloons, and wool hat. The owner, if any, can have said negro, by proving property and paying charges, as the law directs.
D.H. Moore, sheriff Alexander Co., Ill., 31 Aug. 1825

THE ILLINOIS GAZETTE, Shawneetown, IL 24 Sept. 1825
Ran away from the subscriber, near Owingsville, in Bath County, on the night of the 10th inst., a negro man, named Daniel, 23 years old; about 6 feet high; of the ordinary African color; a small scar on the cheek bone, I think under the left eye; had a new fur hat, uncommonly high in the crown; a new pair of shoes; a half worn blue cloth coat; with a velvet collar; a half worn mixed jeans coat; a new blue jeans pair of pantaloons. Is suspected of having stolen and rode off a young chestnut sorrel stallion, tolerable long switch tail, of indifferent appearance, blaze face, and right hind foot white--also a half worn saddle. The above reward will be given for his apprehension out of the state, and half the sum if in the state.
John Crockett. N.B. There also went off with him a young white man of the name of Jonas Warner-- fair haired, low in stature, and about 20 years of age. No other marks recollected. 12 Sept. 1825

THE ILLINOIS GAZETTE, Shawneetown, Ill. 17 Dec. 1825

Was taken up, as runaway slaves, and committed to the jail of this county, two negro men, they say their names are Allen and Ned. Allen is a very bright mulatto, about 5 feet 5 or 6 inches high; remarkably heavy made; he proves to be a shoe maker and house carpenter. He says he belongs to Capt. James Riley, and that he resides in the state of Alabama, Franklin County. Ned is rather advanced in years, about 5 feet 7 or 8 inches high; speaks slow and mild, with cheerful countenance; one of his upper foreteeth has been abstracted. He says he belongs to the heirs of Levin Lane, and that they reside in the state of Alabama, Franklin County. If no owner appears to prove property, and pay charges, within six weeks, they will be hired out agreeable to law.

Vienna, Johnson County, Ill. 6 Nov. 1825

THE ILLINOIS GAZETTE, Shawneetown, Il. 25 Feb. 1826

Ran away on the 22nd January, from on board the steam boat Paragon, near the mouth of Cumberland, while wooding, a negro man, named Lewis; quite black; 5 feet 7 or 8 inches high; 24 or 25 years old; has a scar on his upper lip, and has either lost an upper tooth, or it stands far apart. He had on a white roundabout and pantaloons of jeans. I have heard of him crossing over to the Illinois side of the river, and presume he will make for Golconda, as he has lived there some time heretofore. I will give a reward of $30, if apprehended, and taken to the owner, Benj. Winchester, 9 miles below La Fourche, or to New Orleans to Messrs. Bedford, Breedlove and Robinson, commission merchants or to J.B. Bowles, Louisville--either of whom will pay the expenses of removing him, in addition to the reward.

Benjamin Winchester, 5 Feb. 1826

THE ILLINOIS GAZETTE, Shawneetown, Ill. 13 May 1826

Was committed to the jail of White County, as a runaway on the 22d day of April, a negro, who calls his name John Lewis; about 23 or 24 years of age, near 6 feet high; tolerable black and well made. He says he was raised by one Jaroe (Jarrot) in St. Clair County, Illinois, and if not taken out in six months, will be dealt with agreeable to law.

G.B. Hargrave, sheriff, 27 April 1826

THE ILLINOIS GAZETTE, Shawneetown, Ill. 17 June 1826
     Was committed to jail, in this place, on the 19th inst., a negro man, who calls his name Jack. He is a black fellow, about 5 feet 9 or 10 inches high; between 20 and 25 years of age, has on his left arm a large scar, and very much marked on his back with the whip. He says he belongs to Duncan Steward, of or near New Orleans. If no owner appears, he will be dealt with under the law.
     J. Copland, sheriff, Johnson County, Vienna, 20th March 1826

THE ILLINOIS GAZETTE, Shawneetown, Ill. 8 July 1826
     Ran away from the subscriber, three negro men, of the following description: Bill, about 43 years old, tall and well built, very black, has a long face, and a tolerable flat nose, and mouth, high forehead, inclining to be bald, grey hair and beard, both his big toes turn outwards and make a large knot on the foot, where toes join; speaks quick when spoken to, and with confidence; plays on the violin, and by profession a rough carpenter; his right forefinger was badly mashed, and its marks may be seen. I have understood since he ran off, that he has a free pass which he will no doubt show, if there should be any necessity for it, though it must be a base forgery. Jim, is about 55 years of age, about the same height of Bill, but more slim, walks a little crooked, of a yellowish complexion, speaks low and long, has a peculiarity in his expression, which cannot escape notice; he reads pretty well. I purchased him from Judge Caldwell, near Wheeling, Va., which place he may try to get to. Arnold, is about 19 years old, low and well set, yellowish complexion, speaks short and occasionally has a stoppage in his speech, and a down look. They carried off a variety of clothing, although which were some of drab casinet. I am inclined to think they will endeavor to get to the state of Ohio, as their leader, Bill, has been a great traveller, and believes he can no doubt complete any object of the kind. They also took away a very good rifle gun. I will give the above reward for them, $50 for either of them, and pay reasonable expenses if delivered to me at my house, or a reasonable reward if lodged in a jail, so that I get them.
     Benj'n F. Smith, Chickasaw Agency, 21 June 1826

THE ILLINOIS GAZETTE, Shawneetown, Ill. 15 July 1826

Was committed to my custody on the 2d inst., two negro men, who call their names Billy and Jim, confessing to be runaway slaves. Billy is about 5 feet 10 inches high, 40 or 50 years of age, somewhat bald headed and grey--he says he is a house carpenter, and can play on the violin. Jim is near 6 feet high, raw boned, slender made, about 35 years of age, he has a large scar across his right foot--they have with them sundry articles of clothing, among them a snuff cloth dress coat and a drab great coat. They say that they belong to Benjamin F. Smith of Alabama, about 15 miles southwest of Tuscumbia.

J. Copland, sheriff Johnson County, Vienna, 3d July 1826

THE ILLINOIS GAZETTE, Shawneetown, Ill. 29 July 1826

Was committed to the jail of White County, on the 20th inst., a negro man, who calls his name Tom, about 75 years of age, tolerably black. He says he belongs to one Thomas Duley, who lives in the state of Missouri, and if he is not taken out within six weeks, will be dealt with according to law.

G.B. Hargrave, sheriff White county, 21 July 1826

THE ILLINOIS GAZETTE, Shawneetown, Ill. 5 Aug. 1826

Was committed to the jail of White County as a runaway, a negro man who calls his name, John Hartwell, about 27 years of age, 5 feet 8 or 9 inches high, rather of a yellowish complexion. He says he came from Hardin County, Tennessee, and says he is a free man; he rode a small roan horse 7 or 8 years old; and if he is not taken out within six weeks from this time, he will be dealt with according to law.

G.B. Hargrave, sheriff White County, 26 July 1826

THE ILLINOIS GAZETTE, Shawneetown, Ill. 19 Aug. 1826

Was committed to the jail of White County, on the 9th inst., two negro men, who call their names Taylor and Caleb, and say they belong to William Brock of Kentucky. They are young and tolerably likely, and if not taken out in six weeks, will be dealt with according to law.

G.B. Hargrave, sheriff White County, 11 Aug.

THE ILLINOIS GAZETTE, Shawneetown, Ill. 2 Sept. 1826
    Ran away, July 30, 1826, from the subscriber,
living six miles below Florence, a negro man and his
wife, named Cesar and Viney. Cesar is about 5 feet 11
inches high, stout made, light complexion, 40 years
old, has a large scar on his under lip, by a bite;
when he talks much, he pits more than usual. He has
been shot at in North Carolina for running away. I
think he has some shot covered up about his breast
and on his wrist. Large feet, a piece of one of his
little toes off. He can work at the shoemaking,
coopering, hewing and tray-digging. He is a great
rogue. Viney is 20 years old, tall, stout made, round
faced, full breast, dark complected, large feet,
blunt toes. She may be disguised in men's clothes.
Any person securing them, and putting them in jail,
so that I can get them, shall receive the above
reward. They will be hard to take and ought to be
well secured when caught.
    Nelson P. Jones, Florence, Ala. 8 Aug. 1826

THE ILLINOIS GAZETTE, Shawneetown, Ill. 16 Sept. 1826
    Ran away, about the first of February last,
from the subscriber, living in Franklin County, state
of Alabama, a negro boy, named Cato, 23 years of age;
black complexion; about 5 feet 6 or 7 inches high;
has two scars, one on each side of his face, one of
said scars ranging from the lower part of the ear
towards the mouth, the other on the opposite side,
ranging from the lower part of the ear round between
the under lip and chin; these scars were occasioned
by the cut of a knife in a quarrel with another
negro. He has also six scars on the under part of his
right arm, I think it is, occasioned by his falling
through a loft, and his catching his arm over a
crosscut saw that was across the joists; he has
another scar, I think, on his right side, between his
haunch bone and ribs; it was occasioned by a stab
with a knife, in a quarrel with another negro. His
clothing not known, as I understand he exchanged them
with another negro before he left the neighborhood.
It is possible he may have procured a forged pass.
The above reward will be given for said negro, if
secured in any jail so that I get him again, and all
reasonable charges paid if brought home.
    John I. Bell, 16 Aug. 1826

THE ILLINOIS GAZETTE, Shawneetown, Ill. 16 Sept. 1826
Ran away, or kidnapped, from off the plantation of the subscriber, on Monday, the 4th inst., a bright mulatto boy, named Madison George; about 11 years of age; small of his age; his face somewhat marked from a burn, and sore eyes. Had on, when he disappeared, a muslin shirt, and tow linen pantaloons. When spoken to, is apt to smile. I will give the 80 acres of land that I now reside on, which is my all, and is clear of all incumbrances, for the recovery of the boy, and conviction of the thief--or $10 for the boy alone.
John Lockhart, Gallatin Co., Ill. 8 Sept. 1826

THE ILLINOIS GAZETTE, Shawneetown, Ill. 28 Oct. 1826
Was committed to the jail of Pope County, on the 20th inst. two negro men who call their names, James and John Allen Brothers. James is about 40 years of age, and a shoemaker to trade; about 5 feet 10 inches high. John about 35 or 36 years of age, and about 5 feet 10 inches high, and has a scar on his forehead. They are both likely negroes, yellowish complected; they say they're born free, and raised below New Orleans, and came from on board the Friendship steamboat, at the mouth of Tennessee, 2 months previous to the time of taking up. If they are not taken out within six weeks from this time, they will be dealt with according to law.
Isham Clay, sheriff Pope County, 24 Oct. 1826

THE ILLINOIS GAZETTE, Shawneetown, Ill. 16 Feb. 1828
Three negro fellows ran away from Nashville on the 16th December last, and were seen the next day near Columbia. They were evidently aiming for a free state, but are probably ignorant of courses and places. Stephen is near 32 years of age, 5 feet 8 or 9 inches high, tolerably heavy set, would weight perhaps 180, of black colour. Elijah is 10 years younger, and 2 or 3 inches taller, but not so heavy as Stephen; he is very black, and a little stoop-shouldered. These two boys are brothers; no prominent mark of any kind is recollected upon either of them, except that Stephen's upper teeth are a little wider apart than usual. Elijah speaks rather slower than common. They had good clothes, and one of them carried off two hats with him. They started and were seen the next day in company with a negro named

Orange, belonging to Capt. Doak of Maury County.
Orange is lower than Stephen, and about 35 years old;
his complexion yellow, though not very bright; he has
lost most of his foreteeth. He is very straight, and
speaks quick. I will give $100 for the apprehension
of the two first mentioned, if delivered in Nashville, or confined so that I can get them; and am authorized to pay, Capt. Doak will give $50 for his. Any
information respecting them, addressed to me at Nashville, will be thankfully received.
        J. Bucks

THE ILLINOIS GAZETTE, Shawneetown, Ill. 8 March 1828
        Was committed to the jail of White County, on
the 11th day of February, a negro man, who calls his
name, Reuben Adams. He is a mulatto, 5 feet 8 or 9
inches high. He says he has lived in Abington,
Washington County, Virginia. He had a dove-colored
surtout coat, a blue close bodied coat; his
pantaloons a dark drab. If he is not taken away
within six weeks from the time he was committed, he
will be dealt with according to law.
        G.B. Hargrave, sheriff White County

THE ILLINOIS GAZETTE, Shawneetown, Ill. 15 March 1828
        Ran away from the subscriber, living in Fran-
klin County, state of Alabama, about 36 miles south
of Florence, on Sunday night, the 24th February, two
negroes, to wit: Orange, a negro man, about 22 years
old, tolerably black complexion; about 5 feet 8 or 9
inches high; no particular marks recollected. He is a
likely negro, and rather plausible; had on a suit of
mixed homespun clothes, jeans, worn. He had a quantity of clothing, of various kinds, but is not certain
just much he took with him. The other, a woman,
Orange's wife, named Russey; about 18 or 19 years
old; yellowish, what would be called a dark mulatto;
round full face; rather inclined to be fleshy; she
never had a child; of a middle size, she left home
dressed in a white cotton homespun frock, but she has
also a variety of clothing and may change her dress.
Those negroes were raised by me, and were always
considered confidential servants, and, as such, were
treated more like children than slaves; there has
been no difference or threats of any kind, therefore,
they must have meditated the plan of leaving me some

time before they started, and I suppose their inten-
tion must be to get to some of the free states, and
if so, their most easy mode of travelling will be, by
water down the Tennessee River to the Ohio. I think
it probable they have procured a pass as free persons, from some base fellow, and it not improbable,
that they travel under the protection of some white
man. I would therefore request all persons who should
see such negroes travelling with any man they do not
know, that they would examine them closely before
they permitted them to pass. The above reward will be
given to any person who will take them, and secure
them in jail, so that I get them, provided they are
taken 150 miles or more from my residence, or one
half that sum for either of them, and if they are
taken nearer home than 150 miles, I will pay $50 to
have them secured, so that I get them, or $25 for
either of them.

Benjamin Harris, Florence, 1 March 1828

THE ILLINOIS GAZETTE, Shawneetown, Ill. 27 April 1828

Ran away from the subscriber, on the 29th
March, a negro man, named Bob; trim made; weighs
about 145 pounds; about 20 years of age, slow of
speech, with a down look, had on a short roundabout
coarse cloth coat, considerably worn; casinet pantaloons, also considerably worn; an old jacket, with a
red flannel back; shoes half soled, the heels put on
with nails; middling high crowned hat, half worn. Any
person taking him up, and securing him, so that I can
get him, or confining him at Major Ford's salt works
or in Golconda, shall receive the above reward.

Jesse Thompson, 12 April 1828

THE ILLINOIS GAZETTE, Shawneetown, Ill. 31 May 1828

Ran away from the subscriber, on the 3d September last, a bright mulatto boy, named Madison George;
about 13 years of age; small of his age; his face
somewhat marked from a burn, and sore eyes. When
spoken to, is apt to smile. I will give the above
reward, and very few? thanks, to whoever will bring
him back.

James Hayne, 31 May 1828

THE ILLINOIS GAZETTE, Shawneetown, Ill. 12 July 1828

Ran away from Stephen Douglas log firm, on the

17th June 1828, six miles above the Grand Gulf, on the Louisiana end, five negro men, slave Gino is 5 feet 2 inches high; one ear bit off. Henry is 5 feet 6 inches, 21 years of age. Bill is 22 years, 5 feet 11. All three of the above are dark mulattoes, somewhat yellow complected. Moses is 23 years old, is 5 feet 7 inches, somewhat yellow complected. Any person taking the negroes up, shall have the above reward, if confined in jail so I can get them. This 20th June 1828.

Stephen Douglass. (The previous was written in Egyptian hyeroglyphics, which we found impossible to translate correctly into English.)

THE ILLINOIS GAZETTE, Shawneetown, Ill. 12 July 1828

Was committed in the jail of Edwards County, on the 2d day of June instant, a negro man and woman. The man is a black negro, about 5 feet 7 or 8 inches high, about 28 years of age; has a scar on his forehead above his right eye, stutters little, calls himself Sam and says he belongs to Betsey Coefield, who lives with her uncle, Isaac Coefield, between Salem and Centreville, Livingston County. The woman is about 23 years old, has a flat nose, thick lips, small stature; has the little finger on her right hand so contracted by a scalding burn, as not to be able to open it more than half way. Calls herself Sabrina and says she belongs to Hugh, John and Alexander Dobbins, heirs of John Dobbins, deceased, living about one mile above Buck Creek, in Livingston Co., Ky. They both state that they were hired to Fields Barnet, who keeps a tavern about half way between Salem and Smithland, Livingston County, Ky.

James Jordan, Sheriff Edwards County. 7 June 1828

THE ILLINOIS GAZETTE, Shawneetown, Ill. 27 Sept. 1828

Ran away from the subscriber, on the night of the 29th August last, a negro man, named Horn. He is about 40 years of age, a little over the usual height, has a remarkably high forehead, and is rather inclined to be bald, trim made and of a yellow complexion. He had on, when he went away, nothing but some cotton clothing and a plaid cloak; it is probable, nevertheless, that he has obtained other than that which he took off. It is believed that he has

82

procured an unauthorized pass, and made his way to
Illinois or Indiana. I will give the above reward if
he be taken in Indiana and secured in jail so that I
get him again, $15 if taken in Illinois, and $10 in
this state.
William Waddington, Princeton, Ky. 2 Sept. 1828

THE ILLINOIS GAZETTE, Shawneetown, Ill. 28 Feb. 1829
Ran away from the subscriber in the town of
Nashville, state of Tennessee, on Friday 19 December
last, a negro man slave named Hardy, aged about 25 or
26 years, spare made, a little bow legged, stoops in
his shoulders, and his face a little dished, broad,
with a sharp chin, and small beard, nose rather
large, good teeth, some impediment in his speech,
when he attempts to speak quick, about 5 feet 9, 10
or 11 inches high, weighs about 140 or 150 pounds, no
particular marks or scars recollected. He is a first
rate house or body servant or field hand, pleasant
and affable in his manners, no particular mechanical
trade except being able to make coarse shoes; his
clothes it is unnecessary to attempt to describe, as
it is presumed he will have changed them. It is
expected he will attempt to get to some free state. I
presume he was induced away by some white man. He was
raised in Northampton, N.C. by the late Col. Lawrence
Smith, deceased; has lived several years in Raleigh,
N.C. and in Lauderdale County, Alabama, near Florence
about two years in the county of Henry, near Paris in
the eastern district. $50 reward will be given for
apprehending and securing said fellow in any jail so
that I get him again; or the above reward and all
reasonable expenses paid if delivered to me in this
place.
Rebeccah I. Williams

THE ILLINOIS GAZETTE, Shawneetown, Ill. 20 June 1829
Ran away from the subscriber living on Red
River, Logan County, Ky. on the night of the 6th
inst., a negro man named Thornton, about 22 years of
age, 5 feet 10 or 11 inches high, light complected,
straight and well made, active, talkative, sensible,
and has a good countenance, reads very well and write
a tolerable good hand. had on when he left home, a
dark jeans coat, blue casinet pantaloons, and an old
black fur hat. It is not known that he had any other

clothing with him, but is probable he may have procured others from some of his friends. He was raised by J.J. Mackal, Esq. and has worked a good deal at the blacksmith business; and may be in Mr. Machall's neighborhood, as he has relations living there and in the southern part of Todd County; or he may have gone to Nashville, as he has lived there 2 years. It is probable he has a free pass with him, and may be in company with some white man, and will aim eventually to get to the state of Illinois or Indiana, as he has once made an attempt to go to the Quaker settlement in Indiana. The above reward will be paid for apprehending and confining said negro in any jail in the state of Illinois, Indiana or Ohio, so I get him again, and $50 if taken over 50 miles from home, or $20 if taken in Logan County, Ky. If brought home, all reasonable charges will be paid.

Thos. O. Drane, Logan County, Ky. 9 June 1829

THE ILLINOIS GAZETTE, Shawneetown, Ill. 4 July 1829

Was committed to my charge on the 22d May last, a negro man, calling himself James Matthews, who says he belongs to a Mrs. Susan Buckner of Wythe County, Va. He is a low chunky black fellow, about 25 or 40 years of age. Also on the 23d of May last, a mulatto man calling himself Daniel Ross, tolerably stout, common height, back much scarred with the whip, about 30 years of age, and says he came from Virginia, but cannot tell the name of the county, and belonged to a Mr. Wm. Harrison. Also, at the same time, another negro man, calling his name Isaac Goron, who says he belonged to a Mr. Wm. Robinson, of Virginia, about 5 feet 10 inches high, well set, about 30 or 35 years of age. The above negroes were all taken up in company at the same time, and appear to be well acquainted with Nashville, Tenn. notwithstanding their claim to be Virginians. They were committed to the jail of Gallatin County, on the ground of their not having any certificate of freedom; and unless they shall produce such certificate, or be claimed by their owners within six weeks from the time of their commitment, they will be hired out agreeably to law for the space of one year, when they will be discharged as free, if not claimed by their owners within that time.

M.S. Davenport sheriff Gallatin Co. 8 June 1829

THE ILLINOIS GAZETTE, Shawneetown, Ill. 1 August 1829
     Was kidnapped in the neighborhoods of the Sa-
line, a negro girl, named Maria, about 3 years of
age, dark complexion, nearly black, well grown of her
age, has a dent or small hole in her face just below
the cheek bones, she had strings in her ears, though
the thieves may use the precaution to take them out,
her ear however have been pierced, and they cannot
destroy that mark. The clothes she had on when taken
off were very ragged, and it is presumed will soon be
changed. She was taken from the spring on Saturday
evening the 25th inst. by two ruffians who are un-
known. This girl is one of the negroes emancipated
by the last will and testament of John M'Allister of
Montgomery County, Tennessee, and moved here about a
year ago, and some time last spring some scoundrel
probably one of them stole two horse creatures from
them, and thereby prevented them from making a crop,
and now returned to steal the children, the uncle of
the girl, a black man by the name of Dryas, offers a
reward of $50 for the girl, and subscription is
making up on the girl and one for the thieves, and I
am of opinion that $200 will be raised.
     Leo'd White, Equality, 27th July 1829

THE ILLINOIS GAZETTE, Shawneetown, Ill. 1 August 1829
     On the 2d day of July instant, there was commi-
tted to my custody, as deputy sheriff of Jackson
County, by Joel Manning, a justice of peace in said
county, a dark mulatto man, taken up as runaway slave
or servant under the provisions of the statutes of
this state, who is at this time confined in the jail
of said county. Said runaway is round and full faced,
about 5 feet 10 inches high, between 25 and 30 years
of age, speaks quick and starts when spoken to, has
more beard than colored people usually have. He had
on when committed as aforesaid, a gay colored jean
coat, blue sattinet pantaloons, blue and white
striped cotton vest, an old hat and shoes. He says
that he belongs to a man by the name of Lawson, who
lives in Nottoway County in the state of Virginia,
and that he was on the road with his master between
that place and the state of Alabama when he left him,
about three weeks since, to which latter place his
master was taking him to sell. The owner of said
runaway slave by making application to Jesse Griggs,

sheriff of Jackson County, or myself at Brownsville, proving him to be his property and paying charges, can have him.

Alex. M. Jenkins, deputy sheriff Brownsville, 3 July 1829

THE ILLINOIS GAZETTE, Shawneetown, Ill. 1 August 1829

On the 27th day of July inst. there was committed to my custody, as sheriff of Edwards County, by Joel Churchill, a justice of peace in said county, a negro man, who calls himself Cesar, taken up as a runaway slave under the provisions of the statutes of this state, who is at this time confined in the jail of this county. Said runaway is fleshy, 5 feet 3 1/2 inches high; says he is 50 years old, but is supposed to be about 49; he is marked with a large scar on his right temple and has a pit or hole in his left cheek, which appears to have been occasioned by a rising; had on when taken an old linsey frock coat, once blue, has with him a light or drab colored fustian coat, a grey jeans frock coat, and a pair of blue mixed cassinet pantaloons, all much worn, says he belongs to William Craven, of Cadiz, Trig County, Ky.; had a pass, which he says was given to him by said Craven, but is is signed by John Fisher. Said negro was committed on the ground of his not having any certificate of freedom, and unless he shall produce such certificate or be claimed by his owner within six weeks from the time of his committment, he will be hired out agreeably to law for the space of one year, when he will be discharged as free, if not claimed by his owner.

James Jordan, sheriff Edwards County, Albion, 28 July 1829

ILLINOIS GAZETTE, Shawneetown, Ill. 29 August 1829

Ran away from the subscriber, long 5 miles above Triana, near the Tennessee River, in Madison County, Alabama, on the night of the 5th inst. three negroes, two men and one woman. Bartlett, about 22 years old, common size, black, with some beard; Simon, upward of six feet high, about 21 years old, slender made, with uncommon large feet; Winny, a tall slim black woman, very likely, about 18 years old, formerly belonged to John Rhea, near Fayetteville, Tennessee. I suspect they will attempt to get to some free state. I will

give a reward of $75 to any person who may apprehend
said slaves, if in a free state, and secure them in
any jail so that I get them again, or $20, if taken
in any slave-holding state, or a sum in proportion
for either of them, and all reasonable charges paid,
if delivered to me at the above named place. Address
to me at Huntsville, Alabama.

    James Cooper, 22 Aug. 1829

THE ILLINOIS GAZETTE, Shawneetown, Ill. 19 Sept. 1829
    Was committed to my custody by Irvin Morris,
Esq. on the 31st day of July last, a negro man, who
calls his name Jacob. Said negro was taken up as a
runaway slave and is about 48 years old, 5 feet 10 or
11 inches high, has a scar on his right cheek and
blind of his right eye. Said negro states he belongs
to William Montgomery, at the mouth of White River,
Arkansas Territory. If not taken out in six weeks
will be dealt with agreeably to law.

    S. Copland, sheriff Johnson County, Vienna, 5
Aug. 1829

THE ILLINOIS GAZETTE, Shawneetown, Ill. 19 Sept. 1829
    Was committed to my custody on the 26th of
August inst. 3 negroes, 2 men and 1 woman, who call
their names Bartley, Simon and Winny. Said negroes
were taken up as runaway slaves. Bartley is about 24
years old, 5 feet 6 inches high; Simon is about 22
years old, 6 feet high; Winny is about 20 years old.
Said negroes state they belong to James Cooper, living in the state of Alabama, in Madison County, and
if not taken out in six weeks will be dealt with
agreeably to law.

    A.J. Storm, sheriff Pope County, Golconda, 26
Aug. 1829

THE ILLINOIS GAZETTE, Shawneetown, Ill. 26 Sept. 1829
    Was committed to my charge on the 25th of
August inst. a negro man who calls his name Tony.
Said negro was taken up as a a runaway slave, and is
about 40 or 45 years of age, tolerably black, 5 feet
8 or 9 inches high, has a scar on his breast, says he
is originally from the Spanish country and is a free
man. He was committed to White County jail, on the
ground of his having no certificate of freedom; and
unless he shall produce such certificate or be

claimed by his owner within six weeks from the time
of his committment, will be hired out agreeably to
law for the space of one year, when he will be discharged as free, if not claimed by his owner within
that time.

C.B. Hargrave, sheriff White County, 22 Aug.
1829

THE ILLINOIS GAZETTE, Shawneetown, Ill. 26 Sept. 1829
Runaway negro man, who calls his name Daniel,
was taken up near Mc'Landesborough, Hamilton County,
Ill. on the 15th of August, 1829, was committed to my
charge. Said negro is about 5 feet 6 inches high,
about 35 or 40 years of age, he has a scar on his
right breast which he says was done by the cut of a
knife. Had on when taken an old roundabout coat and a
white hat more than half worn. He says he belongs to
John Lucas of Alabama. The owner is requested to take
him out within six weeks or he will be hired out as
the law directs.

Benjamin Hood, sheriff Hamilton County, Aug. 15

THE ILLINOIS GAZETTE, Shawneetown, Ill. 17 Oct. 1829
Was committed to my custody, on the 29th September, as sheriff of Gallatin County, state of Illinois, a negro man, as a runaway, who calls his name
Alick Stewart, appears to be about 30 years of age, 5
feet 6 or 7 inches high; he says he belongs to the
Indians, and was the property of McIntosh. If he is
not taken out, according to law, in six weeks, he
will be hired out, agreeably to the act of assembly
in such cases made and provided.

M.S. Davenport, sheriff, 10 Oct. 1829

THE ILLINOIS GAZETTE, Shawneetown, Ill. 17 Oct. 1829
Was committed to my custody, on the 9th day of
October, as sheriff of Gallatin County, a negro man,
as a runaway who calls his name George Thomas, and
says he is free; appears to be about 40 years of age,
of a tolerably dark complexion, 5 feet 6 inches high.
If he is not taken out according to law within six
weeks, he will be hired out agreeably to the act of
assembly in such cases made and provided.

M.S. Davenport, sheriff, 12 Oct. 1829

THE ILLINOIS GAZETTE, Shawneetown, Ill. 7 Nov. 1829

My negro man, Barney, who is regularly indentured and bound to serve me agreeably to the constitution and laws of the state, is on the habit of loitering about Shawneetown. I have extended to him great priviledges, and he wishes to take greater. For the future, I wish to treat him as a servant should be treated, and also wish him to treat me as a master; therefore, you are hereby notified, that my man Barney is a servant, and it is my desire that he be treated as such. And if any person harbors him or employs him contrary to law, I will deal with him accordingly. Take notice.

John Choisser, 24 Oct. 1829

THE ILLINOIS GAZETTE, Shawneetown, Ill. 5 Dec. 1829

Ran away, about the latter part of August last, from the subscriber, living at Tuscaloona, Alabama, a black man named Mingo, of middle size, say 5 feet 9 inches high, between 25 and 28 years of age, bright complexion, very thick lips and sharp chin, with a scar upon his face about an inch long, speaks quick, and is a blacksmith by trade. He crossed the Ohio River at the mouth of Tennessee sometime in September last, in company with his wife, who has been taken up and returned to her owner. The above reward will be given to any person who will take up and confine said negro man in some jail in this state so that his owner can get him again.

Samuel B. Ewing, Shawneetown, 28 Nov. 1829

THE ILLINOIS GAZETTE, Shawneetown, Ill. 2 Jan. 1830

On the 8th December inst., was committed to my custody as sheriff of Edwards County, state of Illinois, a negro man who calls himself Bell Tate. Taken up as a runaway slave, who is at this time confined in the jail of this county. Said runaway is about 6 feet 1 1/2 or 2 inches high, and well proportioned to this height, supposed to be about 24 or 25 years of age, his complexion rather light for a negro, has fine features, sharp nose and high forehead, the hair on the front of his head is long and bushy. He says he belongs to David M. Tate, Wilson County, Tennessee. His manners, dress and general appearance, would indicate his having been accustomed to steam boats. If said runaway is not taken out of jail in 6 weeks from the date hereof by his owner or authorized agent, he will be dealt with according to law.

James Jordan, sheriff Edwards County, Albion, 8 Dec. 1829

THE ILLINOIS GAZETTE, Shawneetown, Ill. 6 March 1829

Ran away from the subscriber, living near the Tennessee Iron Works, in Dickson County, Tenn. on the 27th January last, a negro man, by the name of Elijah, about 30 years of age, a very stout able bodied fellow, about 5 feet 10 inches high, of dark yellow complexion, he has a scar or gash on his upper lip, very perceivable, he had on when he eloped a plaid cloak, a blue broadcloth coat, and white woolen pantaloons; he also took with him all of his clothing, not recollected. I will give the above reward if he is taken and confined in any jail out of the state, so that I can get him again, or $25 if taken within the state, and will pay all reasonable charges. The above negro has one or two foreteeth out, in or about the gash as above described.

James M. Ross, Tennessee Iron Works, Feb. 4

THE ILLINOIS GAZETTE, Shawneetown, Ill. 13 March 1830

Was committed to my custody, on this 12th last, a negro man, who calls himself Wilson Thomas. He seems to be about 30 years old, of a sour aspect, about 5 feet 6 or 8 inches high, has a large scar on his forehead, of a dark mulatto complexion, has on a tolerable good fashionable fur hat, a linsey roundabout coat and vest, a blue pair of cloth pantaloons. He has with him various papers, which are no doubt spurious; one of them contains directions from Florence, Alabama, to Detroit, and two others purport to be for his secure passing and repassing to said place, signed Doctor Phillips, who he said lived in or near Florence. He says he was freed in Virginia by his master's last will, who he calls Mr. Kidd, and that Doctor Phillips was his executor, and that he has lost his certificate of his freedom after he had started to this county, and that his present papers were sent to him in its stead. Said negro will be dealt with agreeably to law, until his owner comes and make the requisite proof.

A.J. Storm, sheriff Pope County, 12 Feb. 1830

90

THE ILLINOIS GAZETTE, Shawneetown, Ill. 13 March 1830
     Was committed to my charge, on the 8th day of
February, instant, a negro man, calling himself Charles Edwin Commelian, who says he is free and lives in
Cinncinnati. He is a low slim fellow, rather yellowish complexion, about 5 feet 4 or 5 inches high,
about 30 years of age. He is lame in his hips. He
says it was done by a shot and talks the French
tongue very well. He says that he is a French negro.
He was committed to the jail of Pope County on the
ground of his not having any certificate of freedom,
and unless he shall produce such certificate or be
claimed by his owner, within six weeks from the time
of his committment, he will be hired out, agreeably
to law, for the space of a year, when he will be
discharged as free, if not claimed by his owner
within that time.
     A.J. Storm, sheriff Pope County, 8 Feb. 1830

SPECTATOR, Edwardsville, Ill. 7 December 1822
     Ran away from the subscriber, living in Barren
County, Kentucky, on the main road leading from Nashville to Lexington, my negro slave Brister. He is
about 6 feet high, stout, rough and raw boned; stutters if interrogated or made mad. He took with him a
pair of saddle bas?. It is supposed he has obtained
free papers, and will make his way for some of the
free states, most probably Ohio. I will give the
above reward for the said negro, if delivered to me
in Barren County, or $50 if secured in any jail, so I
get him again.
     E. Haydon, Nov. 2

THE ILLINOIS REPUBLICAN, Shawneetown, Il.3 April 1841
     Ran away from the subscriber, living in Union
County, Kentucky, on the 21st inst., a negro boy,
named Ephraim. Said boy is about 20 years of age,
rather a light black, about 5 feet 7 or 8 inches
high, and stout built; has broad cheeks and mouth;
speaks freely and would weigh about 145 or 150
pounds, and has a small scar over one of his eyes. He
had on a linsey roundabout, negro-cloth pants, considerably worn, an old palmetto hat, and old shoes,
rest not recollected. He also had with him a jeans
dress coat too small for him. I will give $20 for his
apprehension and delivery if taken in this state, or

$50 if taken in any other state, and confined so that
I get him again.

Stanislaus Wathen, March 27, 1841

ILLINOIS REPUBLICAN, Shawneetown, Ill. 17 April 1841

Was committed to my custody, as a runaway
slave, on the 4th of March, last, a negro, of the
following description: about 5 feet 9 inches high, 28
or 29 years old, not very black, says he left his
master on the 2d of March, at a woodyard on the
Mississippi River, near Commercial, calls his name
Lewis, and says his master's name is Andrew Ellis,
and was on his way to Helena, Ark. The owner is
requested to come forward, pay all costs and charges,
and take him away.

Mannor R. Hoopaw, sheriff Alexander Co., Unity,
March 16, 1841

ILLINOIS REPUBLICAN, Shawneetown, Ill. 5 June 1841

Broke jail, in Equality, Gallatin County, and
state of Illinois, on the night of the 31st ultimo,
two white men and three negroes.

Description--George Williams, one of the white
men, is about 6 feet high, dark complexion, black
hair, black eyes, roman nose, spare built, about 35
years old and weighs about 155 pounds.

William Cornelius, the other white man, is
about 5 feet 8 or 9 inches high, spare made, blue
eyes, sandy hair, sallow complexion, lame in the left
foot, weighs about 150 pounds, and is about 33 or 40
years old.

Jacob and Amstead, two of the negro boys, are
black, 22 years of age, round faced, well formed, and
very tall, but very stout, each. It is supposed they
belong to M. Bell, of Patterson Iron Works, Tenn.

Marshall, the other negro boy, is a bright
mulatto, about 20 years old, 5 feet 6 inches high,
weighs about 150 pounds, says he is free and from
Cincinnati.

I will give the above reward to any person or
persons who will secure the above described persons
so that I can get them, or $10 for each.

Both white men were committed to the jail upon
charges of larcency. The community should be on the
look out for said Williams, as he is one of the most
accomplished and daring scoundrels ever at large.

There is no doubt he is connected with a gang of robbers and housebreakers, and was assisted by some of the gang to make his escape.

Thomas Tong, sheriff Gallatin Co., Ill. Equality, June 2, 1841

ILLINOIS REPUBLICAN, Shawneetown, Ill. 9 Oct. 1841

Taken up and committed to the jail of Franklin County, Ill. 1st Oct. 1841, a black boy who calls his name George Washington, 5 feet 10 inches high, weighs about 170 pounds, has a scar on his left chin, had on when taken up a blue jeans coat, gray pantaloons, an old fur hat and one striped and two common domestic shirts, says he is about 25 years old and belongs to a Mr. John Tyler residing in Robinson County, state of Tennessee. Now unless the owner comes forward, proves his property and pays charges, he will be dealt with according to the laws of our state in such cases made and provided for.

Benjamin Smith, sheriff Franklin Co., Ill. 9 Oct. 1841

ILLINOIS REPUBLICAN, Shawneetown, Ill. 16 Oct. 1841

Ranaway from the subscriber, on Saturday the 3d instant, living in Mede County, Kentucky, a bright mulatto boy, about 26 or 27 years of age, about 5 feet 8 or 9 inches high, polite in his manners, uses good language for a negro, plays on the violin and changes his voice when in conversation if excited in any way. He has long straight, coarse, black hair, and generally keeps it well combed, tolerably heavy built to his height. He left in a skiff, and it supposed there is white men with him. I think it probable he will aim to strike through Illinois for Canada. I will give the above reward, if taken out of the state of Kentucky, or $25, if taken in the state, and all reasonable charges paid, so he be lodged in jail so I get him. Letters addressed to me, in regard to the matter, at Leavenworth, Ind. will be thankfully received.

Austin H. Slaughter, 16 Oct. 1841

ILLINOIS REPUBLICAN, Shawneetown, Ill. 23 Oct. 1841

Ranaway from me, living at the mouth of Highland, Union, Ky., on Saturday last, a negro man named Jim, aged about 35, 6 feet high or upwards, is black, spare made, uses uncommonly good language for a negro, is polite and well behaved. I suppose he has a free pass, forged by some one. He is well calculated to deceive, having good sense and some education. I will give the above reward if taken out of Kentucky, beyond one hundred miles, or $50 if taken within the state, or within 100 miles or if lodged in jail and information given so that I get him.

Isham Bridges, mouth of Highland, Ky. 3 Oct. 1841

ILLINOIS REPUBLICAN, Shawneetown, Ill. 27 Nov. 1841

Was committed to my custody, as runaway on the 11th day of Nov. 1841, a negro boy, who calls himself James Young, said negro is about 16 or 17 years of age, quite black, tolerable well grown, stutters when speaking quick, has on brown jersey frock coat and pantaloons, says he belongs to James Young at Dover, Tennessee. If not claimed and taken out of jail within six weeks, he will be hired out according to law to pay jail fees.

Jno. Phipps, sheriff White County, 13 Nov. 1841

ILLINOIS REPUBLICAN, Shawneetown, Ill. 27 Nov. 1841

Was committed to my care as sheriff, a runaway negro man, on the 4th day of Oct. 1841, who calls his name Peter. He is about 50 years of age, 5 feet 10 inches high, dark color, round countenance, had on old cotton pantaloons and roundabout of the same, weighs about 160 pounds. The owner is requested to come and prove his property, or he will be dealt with according to law.

P. Vinyard, sheriff Pope County, Ill. 12 Nov. 1841

ILLINOIS REPUBLICAN, Shawneetown, Ill. 15 Jan. 1842

Was committed to my custody as a runaway, on the 1st day of January 1842, a negro man who calls himself Willis Wilson Thomas, and says he is a free man, said negro is about 50 or 55 years of age, black and 6 feet high, has a large scar on his forehead--if not claimed and taken out of jail within six weeks, he will be hired out according to law to pay jail fees.

Jno. Phipps, sheriff White County, Ill. 6 Jan. 1842

BELLEVILLE ADVOCATE, Belleville, Ill. 18 July 1840
     Runaway slave, was committed to the jail of St.
Clair County, Ill. on Wednesday, the 1st of July
1840, a negro boy, of yellow complexion, who calls
himself William Johnson, about 18 years old, and
about 5 feet high, he states that he was born in New
York City, and came to St. Louis, Missouri with Dr.
G.W. Phillips. The owner is requested to come and
prove property, pay charges and take him away, within
six weeks, or he will be dealt with according to the
laws of the state of Illinois.
     S.B. Chandler, sheriff

DEMOCRAT, Shawneetown, Ill. 19 December 1835
     Ran away from the subscriber, on the 7th of
Sept. last, a negro fellow named Squier, 33 years
old, 6 feet high, of a brown cast, a scar on his left
temple. I bought this fellow from Henry Dickson of
Jefferson City, Missouri. I will give $20 for the
apprehendsion and delivery of him in some jail, so
that I can get him again. I live in Connersville,
Giles County, Tenn.
     James C. Esselman, 12 Dec. 1835

DEMOCRAT, Shawneetown, Ill. 19 December 1835
     Ran away from the subscriber, living in Shelby
County, Tenn., two negroes, Lewis and Sandy. Lewis is
about 25 years old, about 5 feet high, pale black,
appears very humble when spoken to, speaks low, had
on home made clothing, I think said boy is looking in
the neighborhood of Portersville or Randolph, as I
purchased him of John Polk, of Portersville; if not,
he is coming up the river. The other boy, Sandy, ran
off on the 29th Oct., resembles the other boy very
much in complexion and size, and has had the scald
head which makes his hair very thin. I suppose he
will aim for Memphis or Randolph and endeavor to get
on a boat going up the river. I will give the above
reward if taken out of the county and made safe so
that I can get them, or $20 for either taken in the
county.
     Miles W. Goolsley, Shelby County, Tenn. 6 Nov.
1835 Randolph Recorder

ILL. JOURNAL/INTELLIGENCER, Shawneetown, 24 Jan. 1835
     $100 reward for a negro boy by the name of

Frank. Said Frank ran away from Nashville, Tenn. about the 10th of Dec. 1832 and was taken up in Franklin County, Ill. in March 1833 and there served his time as a runaway in jail; changed his name to Isaac Dean, and has been working at different places until the 1st of Dec. last, and from the last information I can get, said boy got on board the steamboat Dove, and went up the river. Said boy is about 27 years of age, 5 feet 6 or 7 inches high, black complexion, has a small red spot in the white of one of his eyes, and small flesh mole on the side of his nose, got scalded at the salt works, Ill., his legs are of a whitish cast nearly to the knee, and weighs about 160 pounds. I will give the above reward for said boy, if secured so that I get him.

Daniel Buie, Davidson County, Tenn.

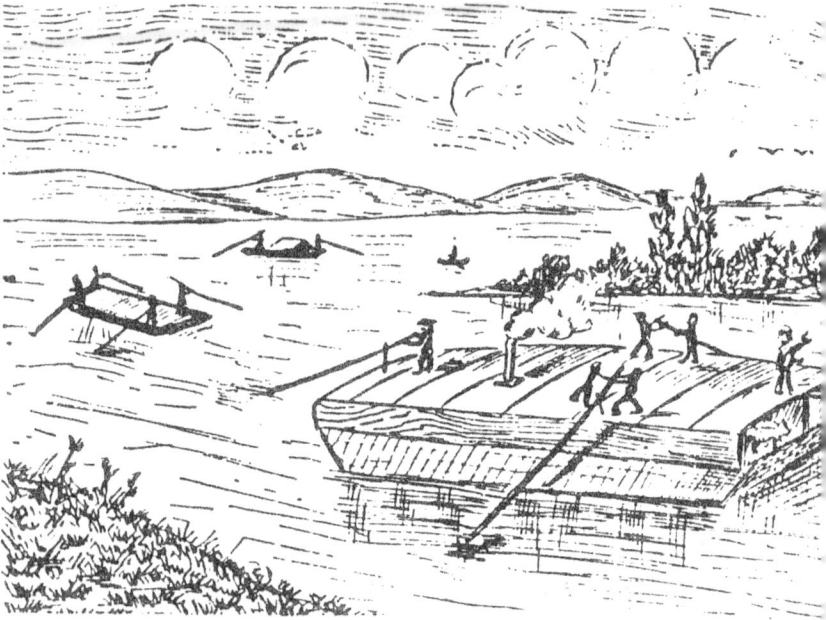

FLAT BOATS.

RIVER ROADS TO FREEDOM
CHAPTER THREE

"All roads lead to Rome." This was equally true
for the Tennessee and Cumberland Rivers. Geographica-
lly, the rivers were excellent accesses for escape--
as evidenced by the given runaway and sheriff notices.
    "...A certain Judge Hall, who wrote in 1828,
    characterized the (Alabama) frontier as the
    retreat...(with) wide-open rivers and river
    country with their easy hiding places and means
    of escape and their abundant flow of goods and
    money...."(Garrett Hist.79)
    On 12 February 1830 sheriff A.J. Storm of Pope
County, Illinois, jailed a runaway--Wilson Thomas--
who had among his personal belongings a paper
outlining directions from Florence, Alabama to
Detroit, Michigan. Besides this item, Thomas also had
"forged" passes. (Illinois Gazette 13 March 1830)
    Detroit, Michigan in 1830 had a population of
2,222; Chicago, 200 or 300. The town of Chicago was
    "platted by the commissioners for the
    Illinois and Michigan Canal in 1829. Although
    there was some speculation in lots at the time,
    no considerable settlement followed and it had a
    population of only 200 or 300 in 1832...."(Flagg
181)(Almanac 221)
    Benjamin Harris of Florence, Alabama in 1828
indicated in the notice for runaways--Orange and
Russey--that "their most easy mode of travelling will
be by water down the Tennessee River to the
Ohio...."(Illinois Gazette 15 March 1828)
    The distance from Florence, Alabama to Paducah,
Kentucky by the Tennessee River was 280 miles; it was
navigable to Florence, "without artifical aid" until
the Muscle Shoals on the other side of Florence.(Enc
Am 26:432)
    Shaped as a horseshoe, the Tennessee River
    "flow(s) in a great bend southwest through the

Great Appalachian Valley, then west near Chattanooga, flow(s) southwest, then north through
north Alabama, and north across Tennessee again-
...The Cumberland River and its tributaries
drain most of middle Tennessee, including the
Nashville Basin...."(Col Lip Gaz 1893)

Florence, Alabama, the stated point of escape
in the 1830 notice was and is on the right bank of
the Tennessee River and 100 miles northwest of Birmi-
ngham. Laid out in 1818, the city of Florence was not
incorporated until 1826.(Col Lip Gaz ?)

"Along the Tennessee River flatboats and
keelboats came into use early....New Orleans was
the logical port for this area and produce
reached there by a long and circuitous
route...."(Garrett Hist 81)

"Flat boats with roofs were sometimes called
arks or Orleans boats. Thadeus M. Harris in his
Journal of a Tour (1803) describes them as
'square, and flat-bottomed; about 40 feet by 15
with sides 6 feet deep; covered with a roof of
thin boards, and accomodated with a fire-place.
They will hold from 200 to 500 barrels of flour.
They require but four hands to navigate them;
carry no sail, and are wafted down by the curre-
nt."(Flagg 152)

Estwick Evans in Pedestrious Tour described the
keelboats as
"constructed like a whale boat, sharp at both
ends; their length is about 70 feet, breadth 10
feet, and they are rowed by two oars at each
end. These boats will carry about 20 tons, and
are worth $200. At the stern of the boat is a
steering oar, which moves like a pivot, and
extends about 12 feet from the stern. These
boats move down the river with great
velocity...."(Flagg 152)

James Jackson, plantation owner on the forks of
the Cypress, as early as 1821, near Florence, Alabama
lost five slaves within a year's time. On one
occasion, Jackson seemed to believe that his slaves
were lured away by another slave--Willis--owned by a
Booker of Columbia.(Illinois Gazette 21 July 1821; 16
Nov. 1822)

Jackson's plantation had a temple type home
with 24 columns; a blacksmith's shop; negro quarters;

carpenter's shop; etc. He never had more than 60 slaves at the Alabama plantation but kept the remainder at his Mississippi plantation.(Garrett Hist 170)

Another confirmation of the Tennessee River's contribution to runaways was given in 1822 by a runaway called Adam who was committed at Shawneetown and he indicated to the local sheriff that he had entered the head waters of the Holston which feed into the Tennessee through Alabama and on north.(Illinois Gazette 4 May 1822)

Other plantation owners in the area of Florence who lost slaves were: Theo W. Cockburn, 1820; J. Cockrill, 1825; Thomas Crittenden, 1821; and Nelson P. Jones, 1826. Jones had purchased the Oaks Plantation in the Colbert Reserve, Alabama in 1824. (Garrett Hist 174)

Huntsville, Alabama was another point of departure. The town was a few miles north of the Tennessee River but early residents of the city were ready to render the Tennessee navigable for larger steamers in 1819.(Betts 36)

"Along the Tennessee River flatboats and keelboats came into use early...When steamboats made their appearance on the river, they terminated their trips at Waterloo, Tuscumbia Landing, Riverton and Florence, depending upon the state of the water level. The first steamboat to go up the river to Florence in 1821 was the OSAGE...."(Garrett Hist 81)

Plantation owners around Huntsville who lost slaves were James Cooper, 1822, and John R. B. Eldridge, 1822.

According to E.C. Betts, during Alabama's first 15 years after statehood-- 1819 to 1834, "the papers carried many advertisements for 'runaway slaves', ...(Betts 53)

However, unlike the notices published in Illinois newspapers, local Alabama papers would not include a physical description of the runaway.

"This for the very sufficient reason that, throughout the entire south, where slavery existed, a more or less competent and comprehensive patrol system was maintained. No slave was permitted off the premises of the master, and only in rare instances out of his slave quarters, without a special permit. Free

99

negroes were scarce, and usually well known....."(Betts 54)

For some reason by 1835, the notices in Alabama newspapers almost disappeared. Apparently the anti-slavery or abolition sentiments had increased to the extent that in 1830, pro-abolition articles were published.(Betts 55-56)

From 1813 to 1827, there were more than 24 known runaways from Tennessee and Kentucky along the Cumberland River.

Montgomery Bell of Cumberland Furnace lost slaves in 1816 and 1820. His runaway in 1816 "descended Cumberland River in a keelboat to the mouth...."(Western Intelligencer 24 July 1816)

John Boyd of Nashville in 1823 also "believed they (his runaways) have gone down the Cumberland River...."(Illinois Gazette 5 July 1823)

Other Nashville area plantation owners who lost slaves were: J. Bucks, 1827; Goerge Smith, 1819; James Atkins, 1819; Robert Baxter, 1823; Henry Ashburn, 1823; Anthony Van Leer, 1822; James H. Williams, 1820; William Murphy, 1820; David Tate, 1830, and James M. Ross, 1829.

Keelboat traffic up the Tennessee and Cumberland Rivers came from the salt works in southern Illinois. There many of the negroes who worked there were from Kentucky and Tennessee.(Hist Gall 21)

"From one to two thousand Negroes, many of them leased from Kentucky and Tennessee owners, worked at the salt wells. They cut trees and hauled wood used in heating the spring water as it moved along a row of twenty to thirty cast-iron kettles. At the end of the line other Negroes scooped salt into barrels, which were made at the scene. From 125 to 280 gallons of water produced a 50 pound bushel of salt and the daily yield ran from 80 to 100 bushels. Hauled by oxen to Shawneetown and reloaded into keel-boats, the salt found a ready market in Indiana, Tennessee, Kentucky and Missouri...."(Howard 132)

The Illinois natural salt wells were near the Saline River not far from Shawneetown, the frequent pickup point for fugitive slaves as evidenced by the notices. The workers at the salt wells were often kidnapped and resold in the south.(Drury 29,31)

"Shawneetown, located on the Ohio about 10 miles below the mouth of the Wabash, was at this time (1825) the principal town of southeastern Illinois. The town was laid out in 1808 on the site of an old Shawnee Indian village and the land office for eastern Illinois was located there in 1812. The salt works on Saline Creek nearby contributed to its prosperity as did also the stream of emigrants from the south to Illinois and Missouri which crossed the Ohio at this point...."(Flagg 176)

Thus the traffic on the rivers was going every whichway on a regular basis. And the fugitive slaves were escaping with or without aid before 1830 and before the later trafficking across Illinois known as the "underground railroad."

THE CONTRABANDS
CHAPTER FOUR

Illinois was still hostile to the free Negro
and the fugitive slave after the inauguration of
President Lincoln. Neither did the state have open
arms since in 1853 additional statutes were passed to
further prohibit any entry by people of color to its
borders.(Cole 333)

During the war, slaves became "contraband"
property of the Federal government or wards so to
speak but were not destined to gain freedom legally
until President Lincoln proclaimed emancipation in
1863.

"In fact, they were treated by the Federals
as free men--...But so many slaves bolted that
Federal Commanders had to set up huge contraband
camps to cope with the exodus."(Channing 136)

Large numbers, then, made their appearance at
Cairo, Illinois, and began to distribute themselves
over the state....(Cole 334)

Cairo became the headquarters and staging area
of a new Federal army under the command of General
Ulysses S. Grant in September 1861.

"The small civilian population--2,200 in
1860--had already been inundated with 8,000
soldiers, and more troops kept arriving by
riverboat and railroad to drill at Fort Defiance
and Camp Smith....

The climate was humid; rats and mosquitoes
spread diseases; and the tenderloin operators
(local business) cheated and even robbed many
soldiers. Worst of all, periodic flooding turned
the town's unpaved streets and troops' bivouacs
into seas of mud...."(Nevin 34)

Cairo was situated upon the alluvial peninsula
between the Ohio and the Mississippi....Most if not

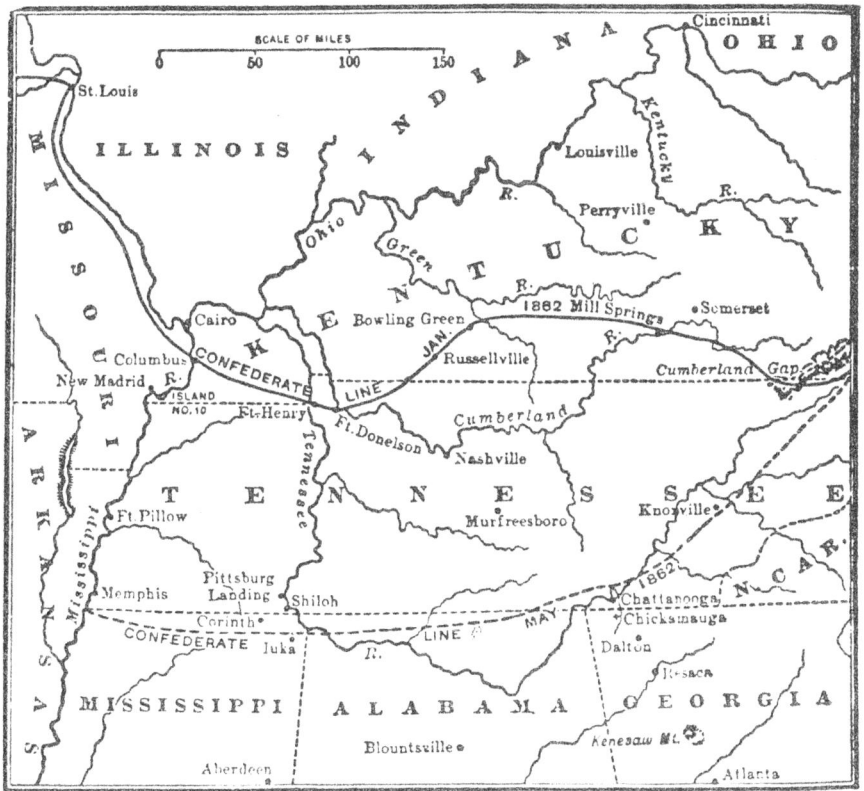

MILITARY SITUATION IN THE WEST, 1862

all the land occupied by the city was lower than the water of the two rivers at higher stages. This necessitated the enclosing of the city with an extensive system of levees. And as an added strategic bonus for the Federals, the Illinois Central Railroad ended its tracks at Cairo after cutting the state of Illinois from north to south.(Smith V 3, 98)

The contrabands, hence, had deplorable conditions as did all the rest. Many of them were loaded into train cars and taken to the north.(Cole 331)

"William Yocum, superintendent of the contrabands at Cairo, was later convicted of selling contrabands back into slavery in Kentucky; a Rev. Rodgers, chaplain of contrabands and Gen. N.B. Buford were also accused of sharing in the profits of such illegal sales...."(Cole 335)

The contraband camp then was only at Cairo for about a year and then General Hurlbut transferred the contraband camp to Island Number 10.(Cole 335)

Island Number 10 had been occupied by the Confederates until after March 1862. Their position there stopped any Federal movement south on the Mississippi until that time. Island Number 10 was in the Mississippi River on a bend below New Madrid, Missouri. It was the tenth island below the Ohio River's juncture with the Mississippi.(Nevin 159)

Cairo was just one of the many locations for the contraband camps. Many of them were supervised by the Sanitary Commission or the Freedmen's Bureau. Monies were not allocated for the

"not less than 20,000 colored persons, freedmen and their families, in a state of complete destitution before the first of December (1865)....The Freedmen's Bureau at first denied the truth of (Josephine R. Griffin's) statements, but further investigation convinced them she was right,...."(Brockett 709)

Conditions for the Negro in Illinois were not much improved, even after the Civil War and the Emancipation. In 1866 at Galesburg, Illinois, the Illinois State Convention of Colored Men convened and released the following resolution:

"Whereas, Taxation without representation is contrary to the genius and spirit of our republican institutions, and

Whereas, the Colored people of the State of

Illinois are taxed for the support of the public schools, and denied, by the laws of the State, the right of sending their children to said schools (fewer than one hundred Negro children then attended Illinois public schools), therefore,

Resolved, That we regard it as a gross usurpation, unjustly shown toward the colored citizens of Illinois, and this Convention do hereby recommend to the colored people of the State to send their petitions to our legislature, asking for the repeal of said law.

Resolved, That our State Legislature, having ratified the amendment to the Constitution of the United States, abolishing slavery, and repealing a part of her black code, giving to the colored men the right to testify in the courts of justice, must be regarded as still remiss in her duty, until she educates the children of three thousand colored men who helped to fill the quota of the State.

Resolved, That to deprive us and our children of this invaluable right (honorably and patriotically defended by the blood of our fathers, brothers and sons), is treating us with wrong and cruel injustice, unheard of in any civilized land or country whose government, national or State, have received the services of black soldiers in defending the liberties of the entire people.

Resolved, That in view of the services rendered by the loyal and patriotic black men of the State of Illinois, during the war which has just ended, wiping from our national escutcheon the foul stain of slavery, that we ask the legislature to give us the free exercise of our inherent right, namely, the elective franchise.

Resolved, That the constitutional disability under which colored men labor in this State, calls loudly for redress; it insults our manhood, and disgraces the name of our great State.

Resolved, That, in spite of every opposition, we recommend to our people the propriety of getting an interest in the soil, believing that there is power in so doing; moreover, to cultivate and improve the same is one of the great means of elevating ourselves and every disfranchised American.

Resolved, That we believe the times require an earnest co-operation of the colored citizens throughout the State in securing a recognition of our rights, as men and citizens, by the next legislature, and that we will unite our efforts with those of our brethren elsewhere in securing the aforesaid end....

Resolved, That our efforts for the achievement of the suffrage question, the admission of our children into public schools, the acquirement of lands, and the raising of stock shall be unceasing; that we feel our manhood, and must exercise it on every occasion, until we are satisfied that the prejudice which now exists against us is done away, and that we shall be treated as men and brethren throughout the State.

Resolved, That as a people whose characteristics are religious, we will continue to preach and pray, and, if necessary, fight against all laws making a difference on account of color, either in Church or State.

Resolved, That we do not ask our white friends to elevate us, but only desire them to give us the same opportunities of elevating ourselves, by admitting us to the right of franchise, and an equal chance for educating ourselves, by opening the doors of their free schools and colleges.

J. Stanley, Cook County
E.R. Williams, Cook County
C.S. Jacobs, Mercer County
Geo. T. Fountain, Adams County
Bryan Smith, Gallatin County
D. Fletcher, Knox County
H. Hicklin, Sangamon County
S.D. Willims, Knox County"

Report of the Committee on Resolutions, Proceedings. Chicago, 1867. Pages 6,7

APPENDIX
ADDITIONAL ILLINOIS SLAVERY DATA

Madison County, Illinois Indentured Servant Register

Benjamin Stephenson, 15 June 1817 registered six negro children: Moriah, 42 days old; Barkeley, 2 years; Debb, 4 years; Winn, 6 years; Frank, 8; and Louisa, 14 years old

23 Oct. 1815, Sam, aged 15, bound to serve 50 years

31 May 1816, Nat, aged 17, bound to serve 35 years

12 May 1817, Willis, aged 16, bound to serve 50 years

12 May 1818, Sarah, aged 19, bound to serve 90 years

29 June 1819, Milly, aged 16, bound to serve 45 years

6 November 1817, Peter, aged 17, bound to serve 99 years

Slave Holders in Madison County in 1814

Ann Bradshaw, 2; Thomas Good, 1; John Jarvis, 1; Thomas Kirkpatrick, 1; Robert Renolds, 1; John Robertson, 2; William Rabb, 2; Jesse Stanker, 2; James Shelton, 1; Joseway Vaughn, 1; Joel Whiteside, 1; William Whiteside, 2.

Slave Holders in Madison County in 1820

William Archer, 1; Henry Cook, 1; Micajah Cox, 1; Ninian Edwards, 3; Isom Gillham, 1; Elizabeth Gingles, 1; James Gray, 5; Jacob Gillham, 1; Henry Hayes, 1; William Hosey, 1; John Harris, 1; Wm. H. Hopkins, 1; Sam Jackson, 1; Jacob Judy, 2; Jepth. Lumpkins, 2; James Mason, 2; Jacob Lupton, 3; Robert Pogue, 2; Joshua Patterson, 1; Alsey Pulum, 3; James Renolds, 1; John Robinson, 2; Thomas Renolds, 3; Benj. Stephenson, 8; Willie Scott, 1; James Shelton, 1; John Todd, 2; Clayton Tiffen, 1, Sarah Vaughn, 1; Emanuel West, 1.

Randolph County, Illinois Indentured Servant Register

14 July 1810, Maria, aged 15, bound to serve 45

years
    8 March 1811, Jean, aged 19, bound to serve 99
years
    19 November 1811, Duncley, aged 16, bound to
serve 40 years
    6 December 1815, Rebecca, aged 16, bound to
serve 40 years
    14 June 1810, Joseph, aged 18 months, bound to
serve 35 years (belonged to Ninian Edwards)
    Jesse B. Thomas, owner, registered the
following: Fanny, aged 20, on Jan. 27, 1809, bound to
serve 11 years and 6 months; Abigail, aged 28, on
Aug. 12, 1813, bound to serve 30 years; James, aged
27, on June 21, 1814, bound to serve 30 years.

NOTE: Some of the other very early counties had
indentured servant or slave registers, but they, the
registers no longer exist.

BIBLIOGRAPHY

Bates, Lucy Womack. Roster of Soldiers & Patriots of
    the American Revolution Buried in Tennessee.
    Revised 1979, Helen Crawford Marsh. Brentwood,
    Tenn.: Tennessee Society NSDAR, 1979.
Bateman, Newton and Paul Selby. Historic Encyclopedia
    of Illinois and Biographical Memoirs. Chicago:
    Munsell Pub. Co., 1917. 2 volumes.
Betts, Edward Chambers. Early History of Huntsville,
    Alabama 1804-1870. Montgomery, Al: The Brown
    Printing Co., 1909. Revised 1916.
Brockett, L.P. M.D. Woman's Work in the Civil War: A
    Record of Heroism, Patriotism and Patience. Co-
    author, Mrs. Mary C. Vaughan. Philadelphia:
    Zeigler, McCurdy & Co., 1867.
Channing, Stephen & Editors of Time-Life Books. The
    Civil War: Confederate Ordeal. Alexandria, VA:
    Time-Life Books, Inc., 1984.
Cole, Arthur Charles. The Era of the Civil War 1848-
    1870. Springfield, IL: Ill. Centennial
    Commission, 1919.
Columbia-Lippencott Gazetteer of the World.Published
    1952.
Cooley, Verna. "Illinois and the Underground Railroad
    to Canada." Transactions of the Illinois State
    Historical Society for the Year 1917.
    Springfield, Ill.: Illinois State Journal,
    1918.
"The Cumberland River." The Encyclopedia Americana.
    Volume 8. New York: Americana Corp., 1957.
Cumings, Samuel. The Western Pilot, Containing Charts
    of the Ohio River and of the
    Mississippi....Cincinnati: N & G Guilford,
    1829.
Davidson, Alexander and Bernard Stuve. A Complete
    History of Illinois from 1673 to 1873.
    Springfield, Ill.: Illinois Journal Co., 1874.
Drury, John. Old Illinois Houses. Springfield, Ill.:
    State of Illinois, 1948.
Dykeman, Wilma and James Stokely. The Border States:

Kentucky, North Carolina, Tennessee, Virginia, West Virginia. New York: Time-Life Books, 1968.

Flagg, Gershom. "Pioneer Letters of Gershom Flagg." Transactions of the Illinois State Historical Society for 1910. Springfield, Ill.:Ill. State Journal, 1912.

Garrett, Jill Knight. A History of Lauderdale Co., AL. Columbia, Tenn., 1964.

Garrett, Jill Knight. "War of 1812 Soldiers in Northwest Alabama and Early Settlers of Lauderdale Co., AL." Natchez Trace Genealogical Society, August 1984.

Gertz, Elmer. "The Black Laws of Illinois." Journal of the Illinois State Historical Society. Vol. LVI, No. 3, August 1963.

Hand, John P. "Negro Slavery in Illinois." Transactions of the Illinois State Historical Society for the Year 1910. Springfield, Ill.: Illinois State Journal, 1912.

Harris, N. Dwight. The History of Negro Servitude in Illinois and of the Slavery Agitation in that State 1719 to 1864. Chicago: A.C. McClurg & Co., 1904.

History of Gallatin, Saline, Hamilton, Franklin & Williamson Counties, Illinois. Chicago: The Goodspeed Pub. Co., 1887.

Howard, Robert P. Illinois: A History of the Prairie State. Grand Rapids, MI.: Wm. B. Eerdmans Pub. Co., 1972.

Langland, James. Editor. National Almanac and Year-Book for 1926. Chicago: Daily News Co., 1926.

Nevin, David and editors of Time-Life Books. The Civil War: The Road to Shiloh. Alexandria, VA: Time-Life Books, Inc., 1983.

Norton, W.T. Editor. Centennial History of Madison Co., Ill. and Its People 1812 to 1912. Vol. I. Chicago: The Lewis Publishing Co., 1912.

Perrin, J. Nick. History of Illinois. Springfield, Ill.: Illinois State Register, 1906.

Saunders, Col. James Edmonds. Early Settlers of Alabama. New Orleans, 1899. Reptd. Baltimore: Genealogical Pub. Co., 1969.

Shepherd, William R. Shepherd's Historical Atlas. 9th Edition. New York: Barnes & Nobles Books, 1973.

Smith, George W. History of Illinois and Her People. Chicago: The American History Society, Inc.,

1927. Six volumes.
State of Illinois. "Act Respecting Free Negroes, Sec. 3." Laws of Illinois, 1819, March 30, 2d Session.
"Tennessee River." The Encyclopedia Americana. Vol. 26. New York: Americana Corp., 1957.
Watkins, Sr. Sylvestre C. "Some of Early Illinois' Free Negroes." Journal of the Illinois State Historical Society. Vol LVI, No. 3, Autumn 1963.

Also numerous microfilm rolls of Illinois newspapers as cited in CHAPTER TWO of this work, available from the Illinois State Historical Library, Springfield, Illinois.

INDEX

Bossier, Baptiste, 55
Bossier, J.B., 56
Bosworth, Bob, 28
Bosworth, C., 28
Bourbon Co., KY, 73
Bourne, Abner, 48
Bourne, Hiram, 48
Bourne, Lewis, 47
Bourne, Tom, 47
Bowles, J.B., 75
Bowling Green, KY, 20
Boyd, Betsy, 40,41
Boyd, John, 41
Boyd, Sawney, 40
Boyes, Henry, 46,72,73
Bradford, Bill, 65
Bradford, Frederick A.,
    65
Bradshaw, Ann, 106
Bradshaw, Ezekiel, 54
Bradshaw, Field, 54
Breckenridge, Jacob, 21
Breedlove, ----, 75
Bridges, Isham, 94
Bridges, Jim, 93
Brock, Caleb, 77
Brock, Taylor, 77
Brock, William, 77
Broisrula, MO, 52
Brooking, Samuel S., 20
Brothers, James, 79
Brothers, John Allen, 79
Brown, Aaron, 24
Brown, Joshua T., 62
Brown, Tom, 62
Brownsville, IL, 86
Brownsville, PA, 50
Buck Creek, KY, 82
Buckner, Susan, 84
Bucks, Elijah, 79
Bucks, J., 80
Bucks, Orange, 80
Bucks, Stephen, 79,80
Buford, Gen. N.B., 103
Buie, Daniel, 96
Burnes, Jess, 46

Burnes, Ranson R.H., 46
Butler, Charles, 46
Cadiz, KY, 86
Cage, Jesse, 61
Cairo, IL, 102,103
Caldwell Co., KY, 15,27,
    37
Caldwell, Jim, 76
Caldwell, Judge, 76
Camp, Abram, 24
Camp, Harry, 24
Camp, Hubbard, 24
Camp, Tom, 24
Camp Smith, 102
Canada, 93
Canton, MO, 48
Cape Girardeau, MO, 28
Carmi, IL, 23,45,71
Carter, Betsey, 20
Carter, Charles, 21
Carter, Dennis, 20
Carter, James, 20
Centreville, KY, 27,82
Chandler, S.B., 95
Chariton, MO, 63,65
Charleston, IL, 3
Charleston, S.C., 33
Chattanooga, TN, 98
Cherokee Nation, 54
Cherry, Anderson, 61
Cherry, Daniel, 61
Chicago, IL, 97
Chickasaw Agency, 76
Chickasaw Bluffs, 21,45
Chilicothe, OH, 50
Chilton, Elijah, 27
Chilton, W. Jr., 27
Chipps, Amos, 21,25,31,45
Choisser, Barney, 89
Christian, Henry, 69
Christian, Robert, 69
Christy, Joe, 58
Christy, S.C., 60
Churchill, Joel, 86
Cincinnati Gazette, 33
Cincinnati Inquistor, 33

Cincinnati, OH, 50,91,92
Cincinnati Spy, 30
Clarey, James, 68
Clarksville, TN, 33,41
Clay, Isham, 61,70,71,
72,79
Clay, Jef, 61
Clay, Joe, 72
Clifton, Edwin, 28
Clifton, John, 27
Clifton, Sam, 27
Cochran, Charles, 72
Cockburn, Charles, 18
Cockburn, Melberry, 18
Cockburn, Sam, 18
Cockburn, Theo W., 18,99
Cockrill, J., 67,99
Coefield, Betsey, 82
Coefield, Isaac, 82
Coefield, Sabrina, 82
Coefield, Sam, 82
Colbert Reserve, AL, 99
Cole, Brookens, 48
Coles Co., IL, 3
Coles, William, 69
Collet, Harry, 55
Collet, Robert, 55
Columbia, AL, 25,98
Columbia, TN, 79
Columbus Gazette, 31
Columbus, MS, 72
Commelian, Charles E., 91
Confederates, 103
Connersville, TN, 95
Contraband, 102,103
Cook, Henry, 106
Cook Co., IL 105
Cooper, Bartley, 87
Cooper, Daniel, 38
Cooper, James, 33,38,87,
99
Cooper, Simon, 87
Cooper, Winny, 87
Copland, James, 69,73,76,
77
Copland, S., 87

Cornelius, William, 92
Corydon, IN, 34
Cotton, Bill, 21
Cotton, Mr., 30
Cotton, William, 24
Covington, IL, 60
Cowden, John, 74
Cox, Benjamin, 44
Cox, Jo, 44
Cox, Micajah, 106
Cox, Thomas, 2
Cox, Winiford, 44
Craven, Cesar, 86
Craven, William, 86
Crittenden, Jack, 22
Crittenden, Thomas, 22,99
Crockett, Daniel, 74
Crockett, John, 74
Culpepper Co., VA, 65
Cumberland Furnace, TN,
18,50,100
Cumberland River, 29,40,
44,50,75,97,98,100
Cypress River, AL, 36,98
Davenport, M.S., 16,88,84
Davidson Co., TN, 21,22,
70,71,96
Daviess Co., KY, 34
Davis, Amasa, 45
Davis, James, 45
Davison, Wiley J., 61
Dean, Isaac, 96
Dearduff, A., 62
Dearduff, Frank, 62
Decoungne, Louis, 52
Detroit, MI, 90,97
Dick & Co., N & J, 16
Dickson Co., TN, 18,33,
38,44,50,72,90
Dickson, Henry, 95
Dickson, Squier, 95
Dismukes, George, 70
Dismukes, Wilson, 70
Doak, Capt., 80
Dobbins, Alexander, 82
Dobbins, Hugh, 82

Dobbins, John, 82
Dorlan, Bob, 42
Dorlan, Clemmens, 43
Dorlan, Jim, 43
Dorlan, John H., 43,44
Dorlan, Lem, 43
Dorlan, Tom, 43
Douglas, Aaron, 67
Douglass, Bill, 82
Douglass, Gino, 82
Douglass, Henry, 82
Douglass, Stephen, 81,82
Dover, TN, 94
Dozier, Isham, 69
Dozier, W.B., 70
Drane, Thos. O., 84
Dryas, ------, 85
Dubois, Henry, 40
Duckson, Douglas, 45
Duley, Thomas, 77
Duley, Tom, 77
Duncan, Joe, 36
Duncan, Wm. T., 37
Dunn, David, 71
Dunn, Tom, 71
Eddyville, KY, 15,27
Edgecombe Co., NC, 18
Edwards, Ninian, 106,107
Edwards Co., IL, 37,42,
    82,86,89,90
Edwardsville, IL, 54
Eldridge, John R.B., 29,
    99
Eldridge, Peggy, 29
Elk Fork of Red River, 50
Elkton, TN, 24
Ellington, Nathan, 3
Ellis, Andrew, 92
Ellis, Lewis, 92
Elmore, John, 62
Emancipation Proclam-
    ation, 13
Emporium, Louisville,
    KY, 29
Equality, IL, 85,92,93
Esselman, James C., 95

Evans, Estwick, 98
Evansville Gazette, 34
Evansville, IN, 62
Ewing, Samuel B., 89
Ewing, Mingo, 89
Fairfax, VA, 21
Falls of Tar River, NC,
    18
Farren, Robert, 21
Fayette Co., KY, 30,31,34
Fayettesville, TN, 25,86
Federals, 103
Fellows, Caleb, 26
Fellows, Fred, 26
Fisher, George, 52
Fisher, John, 86
Flatboats, 98,99
Fletcher, D., 105
Flinn's Ferry, 15
Florence, AL, 18,22,25,
    36,67,78,80,81,83,
    90,97,98,99
Ford, Ben, 46
Ford, James, 47
Ford, Reuben, 46,47
Ford's Salt Works, 81
Forrester, Dick, 16
Fort Defiance, 102
Fort Massac, IL, 25, 54
Fountain, Geo. T., 105
Franklin Co., AL, 18,35,
    66,75,78,80
Franklin Co., IL, 43,44,
    93,96
Franklin Co., MO, 67
Franklin Co., TN, 17
Franklin Intelligencer,
    34
Frankport, IL, 43
Frazer, Geo. W., 15
Frazer, Joseph, 31
Frazer, Nathan, 31
Frazer's Ferry, 15
Freedmen's Bureau, 103
Fugitive Slave Act, 1
Galesburg, IL, 103

Gall, John, 67
Gall, Thomas, 67
Gallatin Co., IL, 16,23,
    46,72,73,79,88,92,
    93,105
Gallatin, TN, 61,84
Gard, Jacob, 17
Gard, Timothy, 17
Gardner, James, 56
Garnsey, David, 16,57
Garnsey, Dick, 16,57
Gassway, Mr., 20
Gatewood, Henry, 33
Giles Co., TN, 95
Gillham, Isom, 106
Gillham, Jacob, 106
Gillis, J.W., 58
Gingles, Elizabeth, 106
Glasgow, KY, 48
Golconda, IL, 21,31,32,
    71,87
Good, Henry, 63
Good, Thomas, 106
Goodrich, Dorothy, 73
Goolsley, Miles W., 95
Goolsley, Sandy, 95
Gorden, Hugh, 63
Gorden, Joshua, 63
Goron, Isaac, 84
Grand Gulf, LA, 82
Grant, Gen. Ulysses, 102
Gray, James, 106
Greene Co., IL, 37
Griffin, Josephine, 103
Griffy, William, 73
Griggs, Jesse, 85
Halifax Co., VA, 31
Hall, James, 46
Hall, Judge, 97
Hall's Mill, TN, 25
Hamilton Co., IL, 46,88
Hannah, James, 24
Hannah, John, 24
Hanny, Amenuel, 60
Hanny, Ishail, 60
Hanson, David, 3

Hanson, George, 3
Hanson, John, 3
Hardin Co., TN, 77
Hargrave, G.B., 71,75,
    77,80,88
Hargrave, Tony, 87
Harlan, Hannah, 28
Harlan, Ned, 28
Harlan, W., 28
Harris, Benjamin, 81,97
Harris, Isom, 59
Harris, Jim, 59
Harris, John, 106
Harris, Orange, 80,97
Harris, Russey, 80,97
Harris, Thadeus, 98
Harrison, Wm., 84
Harrisonville, IL, 55
Hartwell, John, 77
Hay, Daniel, 18,27,32,
    45
Hay, George, 45
Haydon, Brister, 91
Haydon, E., 91
Hayes, Henry, 106
Hayne, James, 81
Hayne, Madison Geo., 81
Hays, John, 47
Hays, Stephen, 47
Haywood Co., TN, 61
Helena, AR, 92
Henderson, KY, 26
Hendersonville, SC, 24
Henry Co., TN, 42,44,83
Herculaneum, MO, 16,57
Herral, Jacob, 17
Hewlett, Harriett, 59
Hicklin, H., 105
Highland River, 93
Hise, Fredric, 50
Hogan, John, 35
Hogg, Jerry, 23
Hogg, Lewis, 24
Holston River, 31,99
Hood, Benjamin, 88
Hoopaw, Mannor, 92

Poke, Charles, 43
Poke, John, 43
Polk, John, 95
Polk, Lewis, 95
Pope Co., IL, 20,21,25,
    45,60,61,70,72,79,
    87,90,91,94
Porter & Co., James, 17
Portersville, TN, 95
Post, Justus, 64
Prairie du Rocher, 55
Prince, Elisha, 17
Prince, Jacob, 17
Prince, Pete, 30
Prince's Ferry, 30
Princeton, KY, 83
Pugh, Mr., 54
Pulum, Alsey, 106
Rabb, William, 106
Rae, Obediah, 53
Railey, Geo., 48
Raleigh, NC, 83
Ramsey, Capt., 64
Ramsey, Jim, 63
Randolph, TN, 95
Randolph Co., IL, 58,59,
    60
Rattan, Nat, 37
Rattan, Thomas, 37
Rawlings, Moses, 26
Rawlings, Tom, 26
Rawls, Hayes, 66
Rawls, Sib, 66
Red River, KY, 83
The Register, KY, 26
Reid, David, 20
Renolds, James, 106
Renolds, Robert, 106
Renolds, Thomas, 106
Republican, AL, 26
Reynolds, Dr. Wm. L., 58
Reynolds, Ivy, 69
Rhea, Bartlett, 86
Rhea, John, 86
Rhea, Simon, 86
Rhea, Winny, 86

Richardson, Ben, 22
Richardson, D.A., 32
Richardson, James, 32,46
Richardson, Wm. P., 23
Riley, Capt. James, 75
Riverton, AL, 99
Robertson, John, 106
Robinson, John, 106
Robinson, , 75
Robinson, Daniel, 35
Robinson, Frank, 35
Robinson, Hardy, 36
Robinson, Wm., 84
Robinson Co., TN, 23,41,
    93
Rockingham Co., VA, 52
Rodgers, Rev., 103
Rogers, Bill, 30
Rogers, Charles, 34
Rogers, Henry, 31
Rogers, Jeremiah, 34
Rose, Dr. Robert H., 29
Ross, Daniel, 84
Ross, Elijah, 90
Ross, James M., 90
Royal, Port, 33
Russell Co., VA, 3
Russelville, KY, 39,50
St. Charles Co., MO, 49,
    63
St. Clair Co., IL, 47,60,
    63,66,68,95
St. Genevieve, MO, 50,52,
    55,56
St. John Point, MO, 53
St. Louis, MO, 53,58,60,
    64,66,95
St. Louis Enquirer, 31,34
St. Michael, MO, 59
Salem, KY, 20,21,82
Saline,,85
Saline River, Creek, 52,
    56,100
Saline Salt Works, 28,71
Sangamon Co., IL, 105
Sanitary Commission, 103

119

Sappington, Mace, 53
Scofield, Adam, 31,99
Scott, Obediah, 56
Scott, Willie, 106
Scott Co., IL, 38
Shawneetown, IL, 15,21,
    22,26,27,30,31,
    32,38,46,66,71,
    73,89,100,101
Shawneetown Gazette, 31,
    33
Shelby, David, 57
Shelby, John, 57
Shelby Co., IL, 3
Shelby Co., TN, 95
Shelton, James, 106
Shippingport, KY, 28
Simmons, Charles, 64
Sisk, Martin, 20
Slanford, Henry, 45
Slaughter, Austin H., 93
Smelser's Ferry, 49
Smith, Arnold, 76
Smith, Benj., 76,77,93
Smith, Bill, 76,77
Smith, Bob, 50
Smith, Bryan, 105
Smith, Col. Lawrence, 83
Smith, George, 63
Smiith, Jim, 77
Smith, John, 24,63
Smith, Maj. David, 50
Smith, Wm., 63
Smithland, KY, 24,29,82
Spectator, 22
Spencer, Randal, 49
Spencer, Robert, 49
Stanker, Jesse, 106
Stanley, J., 105
Steele, John, 68
Stephenson, Barkeley,
    106
Stephenson, Benj., 106
Stephenson, Debb, 106
Stephenson, Frank, 106
Stephenson, Louisa, 106

Stephenson, Moriah, 106
Stephenson, Winn, 106
Steward, Duncan, 76
Steward, Jack, 76
Stewart, Alick, 88
Stone, John, 20
Storm, A.J., 60,87,90,91,
    97
Strickland, Bill, 59
Strickland, Titus, 58
Strother, Charles, 23
Strother, George, 23
Sumner Co., TN, 57,61
Surry Co., VA, 48
Swanegin, Willis, 60
Sydna, Sam'l, 64
Tate, Bell, 89
Tate, David M., 89
Tennessee Iron Works, 33,
    90
Tennessee River, 25,67,
    81,86,89,97,98,99
Terry, James, 41
Terry, Squire, 51
Texas, 16
Thirteenth Amendment, 14
Thomas, Abigail, 107
Thomas, Fanny, 107
Thomas, George, 88
Thomas, James, 107
Thomas, Jesse B., 107
Thomas, Willis Wilson, 94
Thomas, Wilson, 90,97
Thompson, Bob, 81
Thompson, Henry, 68
Thompson, Jesse, 81
Thompson, John, 68
Thomson, Wm., 21
Thurmand, Elisha, 15
Thurmand, Moses, 15
Tiffen, Clayton, 106
Todd, John, 106
Todd Co., KY, 28,84
Tong, Thomas, 93
Town, Ephraim, 59
Trenton, KY, 68

121

www.ingramcontent.com/pod-product-compliance
Lightning Source LLC
Chambersburg PA
CBHW070457090426
42735CB00012B/2582